WARTIME GWR

SERVING THE NATION DURING TWO WORLD WARS

WARTIME
GWR

SERVING THE NATION DURING TWO WORLD WARS

Elaine Arthurs & Felicity Jones

Ian Allan
PUBLISHING

First published 2014

ISBN 978 0 7110 3805 9

© Ian Allan Publishing Ltd 2014

Published by Ian Allan Publishing Ltd, Hersham, Surrey, KT12 4RG.

Printed in Bulgaria

Visit the Ian Allan Publishing website at www.ianallanpublishing.com

Picture Credits
All the photographs in this book are from the archive of STEAM – Museum of the Great Western Railway. Every effort has been made to identify and correctly attribute photographic credits. Should any error have occurred this is entirely unintentional.

FRONT COVER TOP LEFT The Sewing Room at Swindon Works, August 1914 (see page 12)

FRONT COVER CENTRE TOP The GWR Regimental Company Troop of the Royal Engineers at Paddington Station, June 1915 (see page 32)

FRONT COVER TOP RIGHT The 'A' Machine Shop at Swindon Works, November 1917 (see page 24)

FRONT COVER BOTTOM *Bowden Hall* suffers bomb damage after an air raid at Keyham station in April 1941 (see page 100)

BACK COVER A blacked-out Paddington station during August Bank Holiday, 1943 (see page 105)

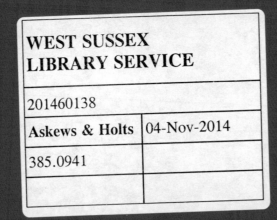

CONTENTS

Acknowledgements 6

Sources and Bibliography 7

Introduction 8

THE FIRST WORLD WAR 10

Swindon Works and the First World War 11

A railway at war 30

Frank Marillier and his ambulance trains 45

Your country needs you 58

Lest we forget 68

THE SECOND WORLD WAR 74

Swindon Works and the Second World War 75

The Great Western under attack 88

And still the railways carry on 110

Women in the line of duty 140

It can now be revealed – after the war 154

ACKNOWLEDGEMENTS

The authors would like to thank a number of people who have helped with, and supported, the compilation of *Wartime GWR*. Thanks are due to STEAM's dedicated team of Library Volunteers who have spent many years sorting and identifying the photographic collection in order to make it an accessible research collection. Particular thanks must be given to both Steve Gregory and Dennis Goucher, who have provided invaluable knowledge and research relating to some of the selected images. Assistance has also come from David Willey at the Bovington Tank Museum, and Andrew Cooper, both of whom provided information and guidance.

While every effort has been made to determine the sources of images reproduced in this book, some are unidentified and all are many years old. We apologise to anyone we may have missed and will ensure that any omissions will be rectified in future editions.

ABOVE During the Second World War the need for new railway line connections, running loops and stations was of high priority. The railway companies often joined forces and new links were built that connected some of the most important and strategic lines in the country providing alternative routes in the event of enemy action. This image from the June 1943 edition of the GWR magazine shows an extended bridge with newly created loops beneath the outer spans on the Berks & Hants line, near Aldermaston. In the early years of the war the GWR was busy constructing new up and down goods loops between Paddington, Wales and the West Country. This quadrupling of the line was of major importance, providing increased facilities for the movement of wartime goods and munitions traffic.

SOURCES AND BIBLIOGRAPHY

A variety of sources have been consulted in the research for this book. STEAM's extensive archive collection provided a wealth of original material such as the War Reports of the General Manager 1914-1919, Works Order Books, The Great War 1914-1918 Statistical Statements and the 1945 booklet, *It Can Now Be Revealed*. Particular note must be given to the *GWR Magazine*, which was published throughout both World Wars. The magazine is a useful source of both statistical information and general railway news.

Listed below are some of the publications consulted during the research for this book.

Adkins et al *A History of GWR Goods Wagons* (David & Charles, Newton Abbot, 1986 Reprinted Ian Allan Publishing, Hersham, 2013)

Bryan, T. *The Great Western at War 1939-1945* (Patrick Stephens Ltd, 1995)

Kelley, P. J. *Road Vehicles of the GWR* (Oxford Publishing Company, Hersham, 2002)

Matheson, R. *The Fair Sex – Women and the Great Western Railway* (Tempus Publishing, Stroud, 2007)

Peck, A. *The Great Western at Swindon Works* (Oxford Publishing Company, Poole, 1983)

Pratt, E. A. *British Railways and the Great War* (Selwyn and Blount Ltd, London, 1921)

The Railway Correspondence and Travel Society *Locomotives of the Great Western Railway* (RCTS, 1968)

Roden, A. *Great Western Railway – A History* (Aurum Press Ltd, London, 2012)

Russell, J. H. *Freight Wagons and Loads in Service on the Great Western Railway and British Railways, Western Region* (Haynes Publishing Group, Sparkford, 1989)

Shurmer, G. and Fenton, M. *Swindon Engineman* (Wild Swan Publications, Didcot, 2006)

INTRODUCTION

The year 2014 marks the 100th anniversary of the start of the First World War. The collection of images in this book not only serves to commemorate this event, but also illustrates the involvement of the Great Western Railway in both the First and the Second World Wars.

All the images in this book come from the archive collection of STEAM – Museum of the Great Western Railway in Swindon. The Museum holds a treasure trove of thousands of fascinating photographs and documents that chart the entire history of the GWR and beyond. It is from this collection that we have specially selected the following images to tell the company's wartime story.

Despite advances in early 20th-century photography, the pictorial record of the GWR's involvement in the First World War is rather sparse. STEAM's collection of First World War images amounts to approximately 150, which is in stark contrast to the hundreds of images taken by the company in the earlier Edwardian period. A combination of Government control on publicity and materials, and a loss of employees through conscription, meant that the GWR was unable to produce the same level of imagery as it had previously done. Despite the lack of photographs, the collection at STEAM does contain some fascinating and detailed written records relating to the GWR's involvement in the war. It is through these records that we are able to bring to life the small amount of

LEFT This notice, issued to staff in June 1942, contains instructions for the use of the new running loops between Kennington Junction and Hinksey signal boxes in Oxford. The instructions were important as, along with the new loops, a new signalling system was introduced that drivers, guards and signalmen needed to familiarise themselves with. The running loops were designed to ease congestion on a busy wartime network and some single loops had a holding capacity of over 100 10-ton wagons.

images that we have. The photographs reveal the role that the GWR played in supporting the Government by the supply and transportation of vehicles and munitions. They also give a valuable insight into how the company continued to operate during such desperate times, and how it recognised the contribution of its employees at the end of the war. It is amazing how much is gained from so little – a truly invaluable collection of images.

In comparison to the few images that STEAM holds for the First World War, the collection of images held for the later conflict is vast, amounting to almost 2,000 photographs. The Second World War collection is a comprehensive catalogue of the work that the GWR undertook for the war effort. The variety of images is very different from those taken during the First World War, this time showing a network under direct attack, the emerging role of women, and the advances in industrial and military technology. What is notable is the increased number of official publicity images that were taken by the company to document its wartime activities. The nature of these images is very positive; they show the stoic spirit of the GWR and its employees. This was very much a 'Keep Calm and Carry On' mentality as staff were, for example, photographed going about their daily duties, but at the same time wearing a gas mask or observing air raid precautions. Many of these images were published in the *GWR Magazine* and were designed to keep up the morale of its workforce. In direct contrast, the GWR also took

ABOVE St Athan Halt was opened in September 1939 to serve the RAF base close to this small village in the Vale of Glamorgan. It was one of many new halts and stations built between 1939 and 1945 to cater for increased wartime traffic. At this time RAF St Athan was home to over 14,000 personnel and was used as a training ground and for aircraft storage and by May 1943 the halt was upgraded to a station as the military traffic to the RAF base increased. During the war, RAF St Athan built a dummy airfield using wood and cardboard just a few miles from their proper field. The original airfield was successfully hidden and the dummy field attacked by the Germans on a number of occasions. The dummy field was rebuilt after every attack!

official photographs that showed a very different side of the war. These showed the twisted wrecks of locomotives and collapsed station buildings that were photographed to document the devastation left after German air raids. These were never published, but were kept within the company archives and are now an invaluable source of information to the railway historian. The whole collection of Second World War images is an array of triumph and disaster, and provides a comprehensive company account of the conflict.

Wartime GWR is the first time such a large and extensive collection of photographs has been brought together to tell the company's wartime story. It features both iconic and unique images from STEAM's collection, some of which are being published in this book for the first time.

THE
FIRST
WORLD
WAR

SWINDON WORKS AND THE FIRST WORLD WAR

The photographs in this chapter highlight the vast range of work that was undertaken at Swindon Works during the First World War. At the turn of the 20th century the Works was in its heyday. In 1902 George Jackson Churchward had taken over from William Dean as the Locomotive, Carriage & Wagon Superintendent, and the Works was busy building a range of locomotives designed by Churchward, including the famous 'City', 'Star' and 'County' classes. The Works was also in a period of expansion, with many new workshops being built or enlarged.

When war was declared in August 1914 Swindon Works, together with other railway factories around the country, was chosen by the Government to be a centre for war manufacture. The Works already possessed a skilled workforce, as well as the majority of equipment, tools and workshop space needed for munitions work and specialist railway vehicle manufacture. Despite the duty to the war effort, Swindon Works also had to continue with normal railway work, which included the manufacture and repair of both locomotives and rolling stock. When the war started it was believed it would be over by Christmas, but as the months rolled by it became evident that it would not end as quickly as first thought. Despite war manufacture and railway work being considered a reserved occupation, more and more men from Swindon enlisted. This put great strain on the Works, which was already working at double capacity. A total of 5,383 men from the town of Swindon went to war, a large majority of whom would have been employed by the Works. As illustrated in a subsequent chapter, the Works relied upon women to take on office-based positions, which in turned freed up some men to work on the shop floor.

The following images show a timeline of work taking place at the Works during the war period. From the photographs, and also wartime order books held in the archive at STEAM, we know that the Works was responsible for the manufacture, supply and repair of ammunition shells, Hotchkiss guns, gun carriages and limbers, bomb casings, textile-based items, road wagons, locomotives and ambulance train carriages (the latter two illustrated in separate chapters).

TOP LEFT The date of this photograph is 7 August 1914, just three days after Britain entered the war. By this date there were already women employed at Swindon Works, and this view of the Sewing Room in the Carriage & Wagon Works shows approximately 30 women working on fabric items for carriages. From Swindon Works war records we know that requests were made from the Government for items such as first aid stretchers, cots and mattresses for ambulance trains, and blankets. These would have come through the Sewing Room to be worked on and completed.

BOTTOM LEFT Another photograph taken on 7 August 1914, and this time it is the Polishing Shop in the Carriage & Wagon Works. French polishing was a skilled trade and from the 1870s women had proven themselves to be highly capable in this role. They were given their own women-only workshop and by the 1890s were officially termed French Polishers, equal to their male counterparts. In December 1916 a directive was sent out to convert part of the Polishing Shop for the manufacture of aeroplanes. Whether or not these women had a part to play in this we do not know, but they would have come in close proximity to this extraordinary sight.

ABOVE This image of the Carriage & Wagon Stamping (No 18) Shop was taken in March 1915. Although no men are in shot, it shows the busy, dirty and hot nature of this workshop. The Stamping Shop made all sorts of components for coaches and wagons, such as draw hooks and brake rigging. During the war the Government requested hundreds of specialised carriages and wagons, and the stamping shop would have been on hand to produce the relevant parts. In the centre of the photograph is a stationary boiler – the source of power for the steam hammers.

ABOVE Another view of No 18 Stamping Shop from March 1915 this time showing the reverse of a stationary boiler. At the bottom left of the image are sheets of metal ready to be heated in the gas furnaces just above. Once heated, the sheet metal is removed to the steam hammers (seen here on the right) and stamped into dies to create components. Incidentally, in July 1915 the book *Life in a Railway Factory* was first published. It was written by Alfred Williams and was his account of life inside Swindon Works. Alfred worked as head Drop-Stamper in this shop for 20 years, until ill health forced him to leave factory life in September 1914.

TOP RIGHT Four 6-inch naval guns are proudly displayed on the tracks outside A Shop, with 'County Tank' No 2232, in steam, just behind. The guns are mounted on carriages with limbers attached. Both carriages and limbers were made at the Works, with the first orders (and subsequent repairs) for various gun carriages by the Government coming through to Swindon in late 1914. This continued until late 1917.

BOTTOM RIGHT This striking image shows a newly made 6-pounder Nordenfelt anti-aircraft gun complete with mounting platform and protective skirting. The manufacturing for all parts of the gun and surrounds was carried out in the Boiler (V) Shop. Some of the old equipment in V Shop was adapted for the deep boring of the gun barrels and breeches, but new machines were also purchased by Swindon Works for the specialised work. Due to the large amount of munitions work required for the war effort, a special arrangement was made for Swindon to purchase equipment and charge it to the Government account.

TOP LEFT Another view of the four naval guns, this time positioned with 'Star' Class locomotive No 4013 *Knight of St Patrick* on show on the turntable. This is very much a publicity photograph for the GWR. Not only does it showcase the manufacturing capabilities of the Works during the war, but it also exhibits the company's premier passenger express locomotive class at that time.

BOTTOM LEFT This is the first of two photographs showing the 6-inch naval guns on display on Macaw B wagons at Swindon Works. The guns were sent in from elsewhere, but the manufacture of 40 large field carriages upon which the guns were mounted was a specialist project that demanded a high standard of machining by skilled staff. This project was allocated

to the GWR by the Ministry of Munitions. It is not surprising therefore that the completed mounted guns were proudly displayed outside the General Offices and photographed by the company.

ABOVE The manufacture of munitions primarily took place in the Swindon locomotive shops, which were well-equipped with the machinery and lifting equipment to undertake this kind of work. The carriages for these 6-inch naval guns were fabricated from heavy riveted plate in the Boiler Shop, while components requiring precise machining were made in the A Machine and O Tool Shops. The final assembly of the carriages and the mounting of the guns took place in A Erecting Shop, presumably making use of the heavy lifting gear available in this area.

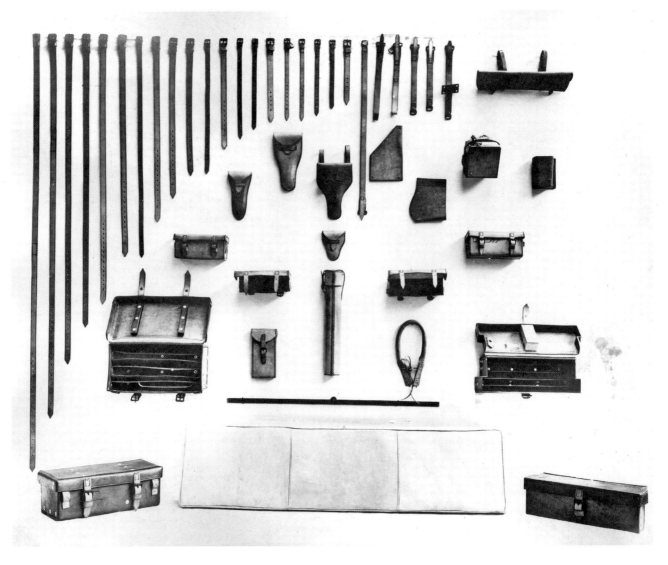

TOP LEFT Macaw B railway wagon No 84350 is photographed here loaded with two gun carriages awaiting dispatch from Swindon Works. The Macaw B was the GWR's standard bogie bolster wagon, which, in normal service, was generally used to transport timber. During the war many of these wagons were requisitioned for military use, as shown by the writing along the side of the wagon specifying 'for military purposes only'; where necessary, modifications and truss strengthening took place in order to accommodate abnormally heavy loads.

BOTTOM LEFT This 8-inch howitzer gun carriage was one of the first batch to be made at Swindon Works. It sits on an unfinished Open B wagon awaiting dispatch. The wagon has had its five-plank body removed and has been branded 'for military traffic

only'. These specially adapted wagons were requested as soon as Britain entered the war in August 1914, with a total of 101 being supplied by Swindon.

ABOVE This array of items shows the type of leatherwork that was undertaken at Swindon Works for both howitzers and 8-pounder guns, as requested by the Royal Arsenal. Twenty-six different sizes of buckles and straps are pictured here, ranging in widths and lengths. Also pictured are a range of different-shaped pouches and cases, presumably used for carrying ammunition, tools and equipment associated with the guns.

TOP LEFT A group of General Service Wagons have been loaded onto railway wagons awaiting transportation. The Mark 5 wagons were used throughout the war to carry food, barbed wire and equipment from military bases and rail depots to the British front line. They were tough, flexible vehicles that, by being hauled by horse, could negotiate terrain that a motor vehicle could not.

BOTTOM LEFT Displayed in this image is a horse-drawn General Service Wagon, Mark 5, which was built by the GWR for war service. The wagon has been photographed in front of the Carriage & Wagon Works offices at Swindon where it was constructed, and displayed on the ground are the metal components of the wagon. This was one of 1,100 such road

wagons built at Swindon Works for general military use. Also built in the carriage and wagon shops were 50 horse-drawn water carts, nearly 3,000 ambulance stretchers and a wealth of other military equipment.

ABOVE This rather sobering photograph, taken in September 1915, shows some 100lb high-explosive aircraft bombs in various states of construction. Two classic pear-shaped bombs with four-finned tails and nose detonators are displayed completed at the front of the image. Behind them are the different components used to make the bombs. Most aircraft bombs at this time were small, usually about 20lb, but heavier ones of more than 1,000lb were also made and would have been designed for maximum impact on bombing raids.

ABOVE A stack of 6-inch high-explosive shells can be seen here piled securely in a bond store at Swindon Works. This image was taken in February 1916 at the height of the Works' shell production. Heavy-duty turning and boring lathes were installed in the Points & Crossing (X) Shop, and during the 2½ years of shell production the Works were producing a staggering 2,500 shells per week. The security and safety of the shells was paramount and bond stores like this were areas where the shells could be stockpiled and catalogued before they were sent off to war.

LEFT This handbook, published in 1916, forms part of the archive collection at STEAM. The cover shows a workshop employee machining a shell as part of the munitions work required by the Government. The handbook contains meticulous engineering details in an attempt to familiarise the reader with the specific processes and tools likely to be used by him in his capacity as a munitions worker at an engineering factory, such as Swindon Works.

ABOVE Two cartloads of shells and shell boxes are being transported around the Works in November 1917 by motorised vans. The shell boxes read 'Property of Shell Committee, Stephen Building, Ottawa, Ontario'. Being part of the British Commonwealth, once Britain was at war so was Canada. In 1914 Canada was a self-governing dominion of the British Empire, but did not control its own foreign affairs. The Shell Committee supplied shells to Britain until late 1915 when it was replaced by the Imperial Munitions Board, which answered solely to Britain. More than half a million Canadians enlisted for service overseas and hundreds more worked on the home front in support of the war.

TOP LEFT This view from November 1917 shows men at work in the 'A' Machine (AM) Shop. As well as machining components for locomotives, the AM Shop also helped manufacture the large field carriages for naval guns and howitzers. Intricate components for the carriages such as cradles, trunnions and actuating gears were machined here to a very high standard.

BOTTOM LEFT This is a rather odd, and an obviously staged, photograph from November 1917. In the records the title of the image is 'Old Forms of Transport', and the men in the picture appear to be demonstrating the old methods of transport that were used around the Works in comparison to the more modern methods as demonstrated in previous images. However, note the

age of the majority of the men pushing the carts. By the date of this photograph more than 5,000 men had gone to war from Swindon, the large majority of whom were young men from the Works.

BELOW This invoice comes from the archive at STEAM and reveals the type of munitions work that was taking place at the Works. The order here, from 1917, is for 56 6-pounder Hotchkiss guns that were used by the Navy and equipped male versions of British tanks. Male tanks carried these bigger 6-pounder guns, whereas the female version carried just machine guns. Note the 12½% superintendence fee that was added to the invoice; this was for the extra supervision and direction needed for this skilled and sensitive work.

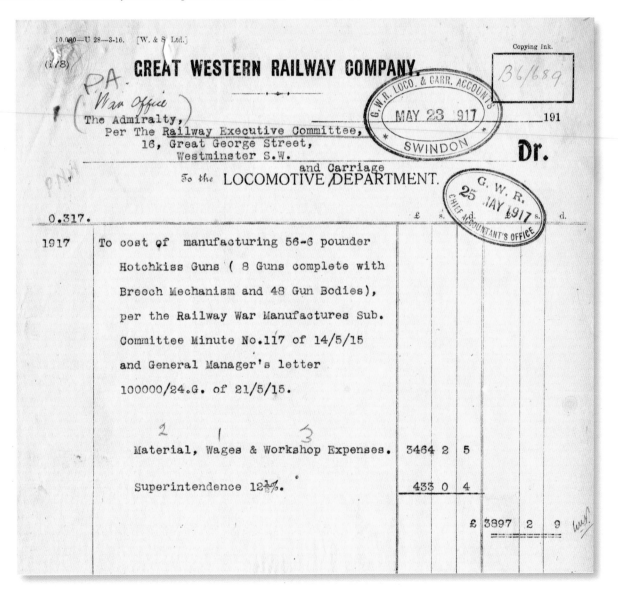

ABOVE This image, taken during the last year of the war, shows the process of lapping the bore of a 6-pounder Hotchkiss gun prior to rifling. This work was carried out in **V Shop** and illustrates the specialist machinery that was required for this type of work. In the centre of the image stand three young-looking men, presumably below the conscription age of 18.

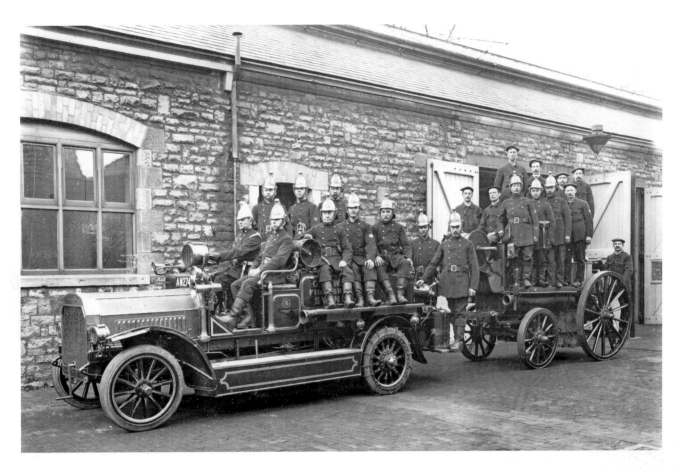

ABOVE This is a really impressive image of the Swindon Works fire brigade, taken in 1916. The smartly uniformed firemen are sitting upon the Dennis Fire Engine that was purchased by the GWR in 1912. Being towed behind is an earlier oil-fired steam fire engine. Being such a large industrial site, Swindon Works had its own dedicated fire brigade in order to react quickly to any emergencies, but during the war the fire brigade took on an extra significance as its members trained and prepared themselves for any potential enemy strikes.

RIGHT The Dennis fire engine is shown here in the large wood store at the rear of Swindon Works in June 1915, taking part in fire extinguisher testing. The water hoses are extended along the ground behind the engine and a small group of managers are watching the proceedings from the side-lines. As the war progressed and air attacks from German Zeppelins and aeroplanes such as the Gotha bombers began to move inland, strategic munitions targets such as Swindon Works were placed on a heightened state of alert.

ABOVE Another photograph showing fire extinguisher testing taking place in the yard of the Works Fire Station in June 1915. This exercise is testing the use of manual fire equipment, with a bucket, which presumably contained sand or water, and a hand-held fire extinguisher being the main methods used.

ABOVE The making of fire extinguishers in K Shop at Swindon Works, as shown in this image taken in 1914, was another of those unusual tasks that the GWR kept in-house. Fire extinguishers would have then been distributed via the Stores to stations, signal boxes and other depots throughout the network. Such fire-fighting equipment proved vital on the night of 31 January 1916 when a bomb attack across the Midlands by hostile aircraft resulted in a fire at Dudley Goods Shed. The fire was quickly extinguished by fire-fighting equipment, saving the building from serious damage. Note also the pile of hand lamp bodies in the foreground.

RIGHT The GWR launched its 'Safety Movement' in early 1914. The principle of the campaign was to encourage a safer working environment for company employees as well as the travelling public. Rather than floundering once the war began, the campaign actually gained momentum and, despite the increase in traffic and the dependency on inexperienced workers standing in for men who had gone off to fight, the number of accidents across the network steadily declined during the war years.

THE "SAFETY" MOVEMENT.

Presented by the
GREAT WESTERN RAILWAY COMPANY
to each of their 80,000 Employees.

A RAILWAY AT WAR

In this chapter we explore the impact that the First World War had across the railway network, looking at images that illustrate the many areas in which the GWR played a vital supporting role in the war effort.

On 4 August 1914 war was declared. The following day the railways were taken under Government control under Clause 16 of the Regulations of the Forces Act 1871, and their involvement in the war had begun. With detailed plans having already been put in place as the threat of war grew prior to August 1914, the first vital task for the railways was to begin moving troops, munitions and supplies from around the country to the coast for shipment overseas, as well as to military training camps throughout England. By the end of September 1914 some 366,560 men and 10,277 officers had been mobilised from GWR stations.

The transportation of ambulance trains, tanks and other heavy munitions, as well as moving vast supplies of coal for the Admiralty, also fell to the railways and created logistical and operational challenges that on the whole the railway companies met without issue. Throughout the duration of the war the GWR ran, in total, more than 88,000 special trains for the conveyance of Government traffic.

From late 1916 British railway companies were called upon to supply locomotives, wagons, track and skilled men for use in France to repair and supplement the rail network there. This was a heavy burden on the rail companies and meant that many domestic services had to be suspended or curtailed, and that ticket prices were increased with the primary purpose of deterring unnecessary travel. By the end of the war the GWR had supplied 95 locomotives, 105 tenders and more than 60,000 wagons, as well as more than 10 ships, for military use.

The impact of the war on the railways was significant. With little investment, staff shortages and the loss of skilled men, increased traffic and the demand for locomotives and infrastructure overseas, the railways were stretched beyond capacity, to the extent that it took many years following the end of the war to recover. Despite this the railways continued their work and provided an essential and specialist service that, there is no doubt, contributed to the ultimate success of the allied forces.

On 11 November 1918 the war ended. From that day the GWR was able to cut back its service for the Government, which took immense pressure off rolling stock, the workforce and the entire GWR network. That is not to say that the company's involvement in the war ended there, as there were many more months of bringing troops, supplies, materials and rolling stock back home before the long process of rebuilding and recovery could begin.

ABOVE Recruiting posters were a popular way of encouraging men to enlist. Millions of posters were produced and displayed up and down the country during the war. The messages were often vivid and graphic, but also very sophisticated; they appealed to the young man and his sense of adventure and duty. The posters in this image were displayed on the cab ramp of Paddington station in 1915. The central poster was designed by Lucy Kemp-Welch, a British artist, and refers to the bombardment of Scarborough, Whitby and Hartlepool by German battleships on 16 December 1914. Both posters were published by the Parliamentary Recruiting Committee.

ABOVE On 18 June 1915 the first contingent of the GWR Regimental Company Troop of the Royal Engineers was enlisted. This image shows that first contingent gathered at Paddington station, headed by a Highland Band, before heading to Scotland Yard for enlistment, then on to Longmoor. In a war report by the General Manager in June 1915 it was noted that this company consisted of six officers, 220 permanent way men, 12 carpenters, six blacksmiths, two cooks, one clerk and one draughtsman, all Great Western employees.

TOP RIGHT This photograph is in the collection at STEAM but little is known about who the men are. Could these six men be the six officers mentioned in the previous caption? From the uniforms we know that they are part of the Royal Engineers and at least three of the men are Lieutenants and one a Captain. They are wearing a classic First World War officer uniform consisting of a Sam Browne belt and cross strap, puttees (ankle strapping), breeches, cuff decoration and of course the obligatory cane.

BOTTOM RIGHT A large group of soldiers are gathered at Ypres, Belgium, in late 1915. Information from the rear of the photograph identifies the lead man on the horse to be a future Hooter Man at Swindon Works, and he is heading a General Service Wagon belonging to the Great Western Company of the Royal Engineers. It is believed that these men belonged to the Wiltshire Fortress Company of the Royal Engineers, a territorial regiment that was involved in building floating bridges over canals on the Western Front. While in Ypres this company came under fire, but from Museum records we know there were minimal casualties to GWR employees on this particular occasion.

TOP LEFT One of the first requests made by the War Office to the Railway Executive was for the supply of armoured trains to be used for the purpose of coastal defence. This image shows the first armoured train at Crewe in December 1914, complete with locomotive, infantry van and gun truck. The infantry vans were converted from GWR 40-ton coal wagons and the locomotive was an 0-6-2 side tank supplied by the Great Northern Railway. The armouring of the vans was undertaken by the London & North Western Railway at its locomotive works in Crewe.

BOTTOM LEFT This image shows the interior of an infantry van from the armoured train. The underframe of each van was made of steel, with half-inch-thick sides and a roof that was three-eights of an inch thick. Rifle loop-holes with sliding doors can be seen on each side of the van. When fully equipped the vans were fitted out with folding tables, lockers, drinking water tanks, a cooking stove and rifle racks.

BELOW This wagon was specially constructed for the transportation of aeroplanes in cases, particularly dismantled fuselages and wings. The Gadfly was converted in 1917 at Swindon Works from old carriage underframes, with No 94679 (pictured) converted from an 1889 Beaver flat wagon. At the start of the war aeroplanes were in their infancy, but by the end they had gone from basic and crude flying machines to a

relatively sophisticated technology. They were involved in air-to-air combat, bombing missions and, most crucially, strategic aerial photography.

BELOW This open goods wagon has been converted for the military at Swindon Works for carrying horses. Horses were an integral part of the war effort; they were vital forms of transport and were used in carrying goods. As early as October 1914 Frank Potter, the GWR's General Manager, reported that the Government had requested the GWR to supply its own horses at cost price for the war effort. At that time 273 of the company's horses were requisitioned. A staggering 8 million horses, donkeys and mules lost their lives during the First World War.

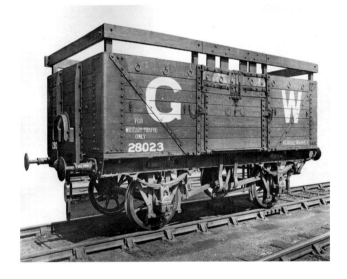

G. W. R. S. S. Reindeer, Jersey. Printed in Belgium.

LEFT Before the war the Great Western steamers SS *Reindeer* and SS *Roebuck* were part of the company's Weymouth passenger fleet and operated the Channel Island services. At the outbreak of war the Admiralty commandeered a number of GWR steamers, which included the two pictured here. Both the *Roebuck* and the *Reindeer* served as minesweepers, with the former being renamed HMS *Roedean* on her conversion. On 13 January 1915 she dragged anchor at Scapa Flow and sank during a collision with the repair hulk *Imperious*, becoming the first railway ship to be lost on war service. SS *Reindeer* continued to serve throughout the war in the Mediterranean and was eventually returned to the company for normal service.

ABOVE In late 1916 a call came from the Director General of Transportation in France for significant numbers of locomotives, trucks and track to be sent to France immediately. The French railway infrastructure had suffered heavy losses during occupation, and in order to fight an effective battle the means to mobilise munitions and troops around the country was essential. Britain's railway companies were asked to supply between them approximately 350 locomotives and up to 20,000 trucks. One of the many engines that the GWR supplied during 1917 to be sent for operation in France was 2-6-0 No 5319, pictured here in later years with its crew.

TOP In its first consignment of locomotives destined for France, the GWR supplied 72 engines from the 0-6-0 'Dean Goods' class, and subsequent batches of 0-6-0 and 2-6-0 locomotives followed. 'Dean Goods' No 2463, pictured here, was one of those shipped over to the Western Front to work hauling ammunition trains. The loss of a significant amount of locomotives abroad had serious implications for the operation of the railways in Britain, not least because of the extent of munitions and troop movements taking place on home soil, in addition to the day-to-day business of the operating companies.

ABOVE The North British Locomotive Co built Railway Operating Division (ROD) locomotive No 1961, latterly GWR locomotive No 3066, is pictured here with its ROD number emblazoned on the side of the tender. All of the locomotives that were sent overseas were allocated to the ROD of the Royal Engineers. As the war continued so too did the need for locomotives in Europe, and it was clear that the ROD needed its own standard locomotive. The 2-8-0 class of locomotive was the one that was adopted for this purpose and, although the original design was based on the Great Central Railway's Class '8K' 2-8-0, the GWR, together with the other major railway companies, committed to building them.

TOP Here is another 2-8-0 ROD locomotive, seen at Swindon Works in July 1921. Again, this locomotive was built by the North British Locomotive Co as engine No 1868, and was then taken on loan by the GWR after the war and allocated the number 3084. What is particularly interesting about this image is the fact that the engine is displaying both its ROD and GWR number plates on the side of the cab.

ABOVE ROD locomotive No 2155, subsequently renumbered 3043 by the GWR, hauls a goods train through Swindon Junction station following the end of the war. Once their service in Europe came to an end many ROD 2-8-0 locomotives were either loaned or sold to British railway companies for operation on home soil. The GWR purchased 20 in 1919 and another 80, including No 3043, in 1925. These locomotives were converted into '3000' Class engines and were predominantly used for heavy freight traffic across the entire Great Western network.

ABOVE This photograph of Straker Squire 1-ton parcels van No 142 was taken in Cardiff to illustrate the large gas bag that was strapped to the top of it. From early 1918 many passenger road services were suspended due to petrol shortages and, in an attempt to address this issue, a number of GWR road vehicles, including the company's smaller parcel vans, were adapted to run on coal gas. The pipe running along the side of the body of this van drew the gas from the bag on the roof to the engine. Approximately 250 cubic metres of gas provided power equivalent to 1 gallon of petrol.

LEFT This posed picture taken in April 1916 shows a driver from the Road Motor Department. The role of the motor driver was not always easy, being exposed to all winds and weather in open-sided vehicles. They were also expected to be proficient car mechanics, able to carry out repairs at the side of the road in the event of a breakdown. But the biggest challenge to the driver of those vehicles converted to run on coal gas was keeping the gas bag secured to the vehicle in very windy weather when they were known to break free from the strapping and blow away.

BELOW American Expeditionary Forces are photographed disembarking from SS *Miltiades*, which is berthed at the GWR's Newport Docks circa 1917. The soldiers are easily recognisable among the crowds of civilians and dock workers by their distinctive campaign hats. A group of soldiers is already on dry land holding two rolled-up regimental flags, while many more can be seen looking out at the activity on the dock below from the middle and lower decks of the ship.

TOP LEFT This series of three images shows tanks being loaded onto Swindon-built Rectank wagons in 1918. The Rectank wagon was specially built to carry tanks and other armoured fighting vehicles to a capacity of 35 and 40 tons, and allowed tanks to be driven up to a wagon and loaded at ground level. Previous to this, tanks had to be craned onto railway wagons to be transported.

BOTTOM LEFT This image shows a tank fully loaded onto the Rectank wagons. The tank is actually crossing over the buffers of two Rectank wagons and could manoeuvre lengthways to allow more tanks to be loaded. The tank and wagons are surrounded by a group of military personnel and officers from the British Army and Royal Navy.

ABOVE The final image shows tank No 9771 loaded on a Rectank wagon. This tank, together with No. 9767 (the latter pictured in the previous two images), is a Mark V* female tank that first saw action in the summer of 1918. The face of a naval officer can be seen at the small hatch in the front. The Royal Navy was heavily involved with tanks during the First World War; it tested and certified new tanks and was involved in the shipping and safe passage of tanks to France.

ABOVE This shot captures the last servicemen to be offered refreshments at the Soldiers and Sailors Free Buffet at Paddington station on 28 June 1919. The forces canteen opened in April 1915 to offer sustenance to the servicemen who passed through Paddington during the war years. It was staffed day and night by a dedicated group of more than 80 female volunteers who, during the four years that it was open, served refreshments to more than 3 million men. The soldier sitting in the corner seat was himself a Great Western man, possibly on his journey home from active duty.

RIGHT This photograph featured in the *GWR Magazine* in April 1918 and shows Mrs J. J. Runge, who was superintendent in charge of the Soldiers and Sailors Free Buffet at Paddington. Mrs Runge can also be seen in the previous image, serving at the counter alongside some of the many women she enlisted to help run the canteen. It was due to her effort and organisation that the Free Buffet provided a vital service during the war years, and in 1918 she was awarded an OBE in recognition of her hard work and dedication.

FRANK MARILLIER AND HIS AMBULANCE TRAINS

The majority of images in this section come from a set of two very attractive photograph albums held in the collection at STEAM, containing more than 80 official GWR photographs from the First World War. These images of ambulance trains, built at Swindon Works, are a fascinating record of how they were constructed and furnished, and the subsequent complexities of transporting them to the continent.

In total the GWR supplied and constructed 16 ambulance trains out of the 69 used on both the home front and abroad. This equated to 256 carriages. Orders for ambulance trains came in almost immediately, as transport for war casualties was of high priority. From August 1914 until July 1918 the GWR took orders from the Government for a range

of carriages for both British and United States troops. Frank Marillier and his team at the Carriage & Wagon Works worked tirelessly to supply, build and repair ambulance trains at Swindon, as well as continuing to build and maintain carriages for use on the GWR passenger network.

The horrors of the First World War are well documented. More than 900,000 men from Britain and the British Empire were killed in action, with up to 2 million men wounded. The ambulance trains played a vital role in transporting the casualties to military hospitals on the Western Front and back in Britain. Had these trains not been in operation, or failed to be delivered on time, the statistics could have been worse.

LEFT Frank William Marillier is perhaps one of the unsung heroes of the First World War. During the war he was the Carriage & Wagon Works Manager at Swindon. At the outbreak of war the Government requested the build and supply of a large number of ambulance trains. Marillier became directly involved in the modification of GWR 'Toplight' carriages into ambulance carriages and designed many of their interior fixtures and fittings. One of the most notable features he designed was the three-tier folding bunk system – illustrated in the following photographs. Marillier was awarded the OBE in 1918 for Services to Munitions, then in 1920 he was awarded the CBE.

BELOW This photograph, taken in September 1914, shows four military personnel demonstrating the loading of a patient on a stretcher into one of the carriages of Ambulance Train No 4. The carriages were assembled and supplied by the GWR and were part of a nine-vehicle train used for service on the home front. The vehicles carried the wounded and sick from British ports to military hospitals.

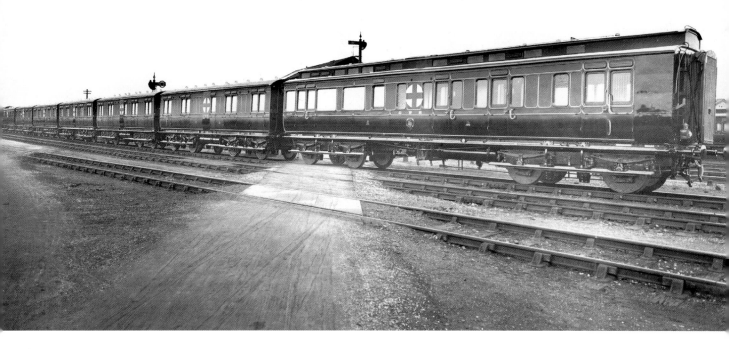

ABOVE Another view of Ambulance Train No 4, in formation outside Swindon Works. The train consisted of nine eight-wheeled vehicles, which included a saloon car with store; a restaurant car; four ward coaches with beds for 18 men; a pharmacy coach with operating room; a second saloon with beds for officer patients and accommodation for doctors and nurses; and a final ward coach with beds for four officers and 14 men.

BELOW Carriage No 9024, a former invalid coach, is suspended in the Carriage Lifting Shop at Swindon Works. The date is March 1915 and the carriage is being converted into a military ambulance train. A red cross can be seen on the side of the vehicle and another cross would have been painted on the roof. It is also noted that the carriage is fitted with a Westinghouse brake system, in addition to a vacuum brake; this was an essential fitting and allowed the carriage to run over any railway in the country.

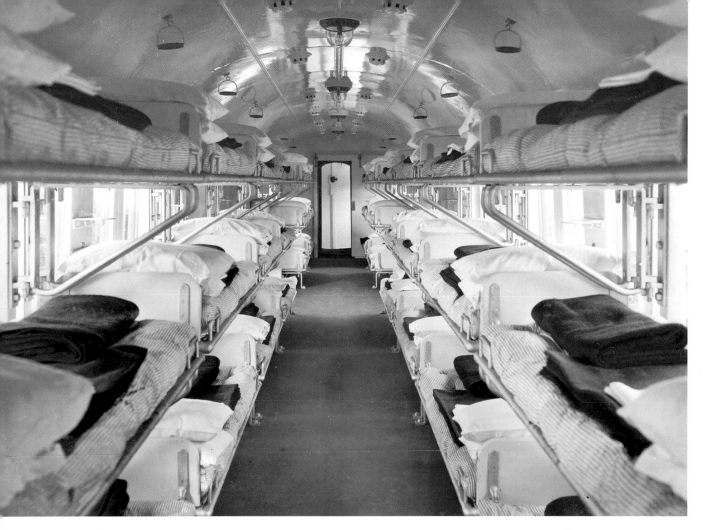

TOP LEFT This interior shot of a ward coach from Ambulance Train No 16 shows the three-tier folding bunk system designed by Frank Marillier. This novel design allowed the ward coach to accommodate lying-down patients as well as providing comfortable travel for those patients who could sit up; the central bunk folded down to provide a back rest to the bottom bunk, allowing a seated position for less seriously wounded patients.

BOTTOM LEFT This view shows the central bunk folded down to accommodate seated patients. The three-tier bunk system was designed for the continental ambulance trains, of which No 16 was one. It was built from new by the GWR and entered service in France in April 1915. The cost of building the carriages from new was approximately £12,500 and was paid for by the United Kingdom Flour Millers' Association.

ABOVE Another shot of Ambulance Train No 16 shows the kitchen car. A plaque can be seen on the door, recognising the generosity of the United Kingdom Flour Millers' Association in paying for the train. GWR Inspector Godsell, a foreman and loading expert from Swindon, and eight of his men supervised the transportation of this train to France.

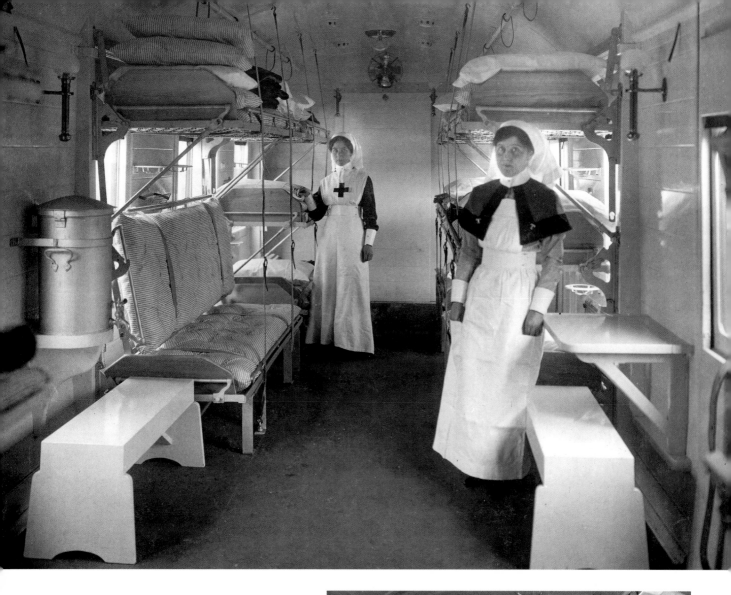

RIGHT This rather stark image shows the basic treatment room of the pharmacy car belonging to Ambulance Train No 20, which was supplied by the GWR for use on the home front. From archive material at STEAM it is known that the types of injuries and illnesses sustained by men in the war were extremely varied, ranging from shrapnel and bullet wounds to fractured skulls, and from frostbite to typhoid fever. The treatment rooms of all ambulance trains would have seen a multitude of harrowing cases.

LEFT Two nurses pose in a ward car, part of Ambulance Train No 18. This train was constructed by the GWR in 1915 for use on the continent and saw service in both France and Italy. It consisted of 16 coaches and was 960 feet in length. Before it entered service, No 18 was on display at Paddington station for three days, and more than 4,000 people paid to see it, the proceeds going towards War Funds. A set of four postcards showing Ambulance Train No 18 was also produced to raise funds, this image being part of the set.

BELOW Another invoice from the archive at STEAM, this time for the preparation of additional coaches for four ambulance trains for the home front in 1917. The invoice has been broken down into sections, the final total being £3,436 1s 11d – the equivalent to about £150,000 at today's values. This was just one invoice sent to the War Office, from one railway company. The bill for the Government would have eventually run into millions.

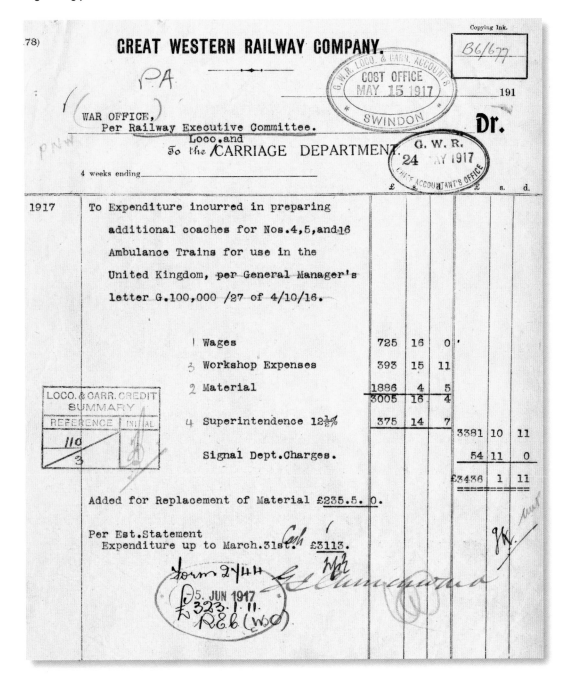

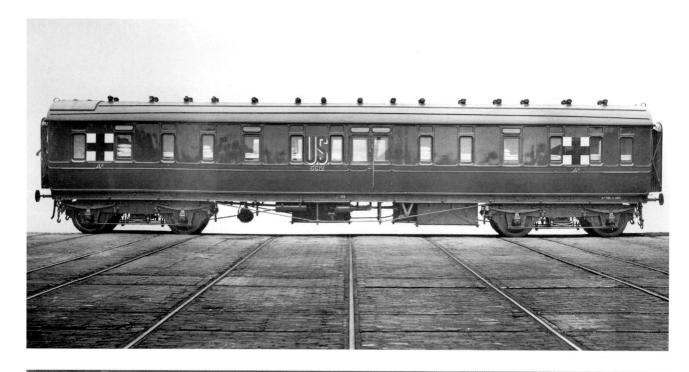

TOP LEFT The United States of America entered the First World War in April 1917, with troops arriving in Britain and France later that year. But it was not until 1918 that the USA played a more active role in the war. Like the British, the Americans also needed their own ambulance trains to convey sick and injured soldiers. This image shows a ward car of US Ambulance Train No 55, which was completed at Swindon Works in early 1918. The ward cars were very similar to the British design and also carried Marillier's three-tier folding bunk system.

BOTTOM LEFT In contrast to the internal views of the previous ward cars, this shot of the Sitting Sick Officers car of US Ambulance Train No 55 shows more comfortable and stylish surroundings. Leather seats, flowers on the table and mirrors were luxuries only afforded to officers of a certain level. The most a patient in the ward car could hope for was a paper rack, ash tray and cup holder.

ABOVE This formal shot shows Inspector Godsell (standing, centre) and eight GWR employees. As already mentioned, Inspector Godsell and his men were involved in the transportation of ambulance trains from Britain to France. This involved some precarious cross-Channel transits, including being on the SS *Africa* when it was mined by a German submarine while on its way to France. For his expertise in transporting heavy and exceptional loads for the war effort, Inspector Godsell was awarded an MBE in 1918.

ABOVE These four images show the process of lifting and manoeuvring that was undertaken by Inspector Godsell and his team to transport the ambulance trains to the coast and on to France. This first shows a coach of Ambulance Train No 16 being lifted outside of the General Offices at Swindon Works. Various methods were trialled before shipment to the continent in order to carry out the most efficient lift while at port.

LEFT A large crane lifts an ambulance train carriage at Tilbury Docks in Essex. Underneath the carriage is a large group of men, which probably includes Inspector Godsell and his team. Health & safety was obviously not a consideration in those days judging by the nonchalance of the men standing around!

TOP RIGHT A side view of an ambulance train carriage as it is lifted by crane at Tilbury Docks. The two girders that form part of the lifting mechanism are clearly marked GWR Swindon. This was the most successful method of lifting that was trialled at Swindon Works and the specialist lifting girders accompanied the trains on their journey.

ABOVE This final image of the set shows the ambulance carriages fully loaded on the SS *Africa*, a British cargo steamship. On 16 September 1915, while transporting ambulance trains to Boulogne, the ship was mined by German submarine UC-6 just off the coast of Kent, near Deal. Two of the crew were killed by the explosion, but the other men on board, including Inspector Godsell and other GWR employees, survived. Despite the incident occurring close to the coast, the ambulance carriages could not be salvaged.

ABOVE As well as transporting ambulance trains via cargo ship, the carriages were also shipped on cross-Channel ferries. This image from early 1918 shows the deck of a ferry at Southampton equipped with tracks in preparation for loading railway vehicles. On either side of the tracks stand a number of War Department trucks that had been bought by the Government from the American-based Peerless Motor Car Company.

ABOVE A second view of the Southampton ferry, this time showing US continental ambulance carriages loaded on deck. The direct link to the port by rail, and using rails on board the ferry, allowed for smoother and quicker transportation. Of the 800 or more ambulance trains distributed by the British railway companies to the continent, only four failed to reach their destination.

YOUR COUNTRY NEEDS YOU

After the declaration of war in August 1914 the Secretary of State for War, Lord Kitchener, issued a call for volunteers to join the Army. More than 7,000 men from the Great Western Railway took heed and signed up in the first couple of months, and this had risen to 15,263 by the end of 1915. As the war's momentum built it was obvious that more men were needed to increase the size of the Armed Forces. A new call for voluntary attestation under the Derby Scheme in late 1915 was disappointing, and in 1916 all voluntary enlistment was stopped with the introduction of the Military Service Act. Compulsory enlistment, or conscription, now meant that both single and married men aged 18 to 41 (increasing to 51 in 1918) were eligible for service. The number of Great Western men who enlisted steadily rose, and by the end of the war in November 1918 the total number of employees who had joined the Colours stood at 25,479, which equated to 32.6% of the company in its pre-war capacity.

The GWR was greatly affected by the sudden loss of its men to the war. Not only was the company required to keep its own railway functioning, but it was also assigned new responsibilities from the Government. Some railway occupations allowed men to become exempt from enlistment should the company wish; they were those essential to the efficient working of the railway and the manufacture of munitions, including enginemen, firemen, signalmen, shunters and high-grade goods workers.

However, despite this, huge gaps began to appear in the workforce.

In order to fill these employment gaps the GWR took the initiative to employ a number of staff on temporary contracts. In addition to this it also utilised the skills of former employees who had retired. But one of the most profound moves by the GWR was the mass employment of women, particularly in roles normally associated with male members of staff. At the start of the war the GWR employed a total of 1,371 women and girls, but by August 1918 this had risen to 6,345. In some roles, such as ticket collecting and carriage cleaning, the women outnumbered the men. However, despite this move towards female inclusion the GWR was not as forward thinking as some of the other railway companies. There is very little evidence of women being employed on the shop floor at Swindon Works other than in the roles they had before the war. A brief mention of women working as labourers at Swindon Works was made by General Manager Frank Potter in his war report of November 1916, but this appears to have been opposed by some men and the subject forgotten. Elsewhere in the country other railway companies employed women to work on the manufacture of both munitions and locomotives.

The accompanying images are a snapshot of the men and women who were employed by the GWR for the duration of the war.

ABOVE This image of female clerks was taken in May 1916, just 10 years after women were first employed in clerical positions within the GWR. They belonged to the Chief Mechanical Engineers Office in Swindon and were managed by the Chief Clerk, Mr Lockyer. During the war the number of women becoming clerks increased as positions became vacant, but it was not without disapproving observations. In December 1915 a Mr J. R. Bennett wrote an article in the *GWR Magazine* criticising certain qualities of female clerks. This provoked a lively debate and in January 1916 the magazine published two responses from female employees. The debate rumbled on until late 1917 when a rather stern and educated response in favour of female clerks was made by Dorothy R. Dalton, B.A!

ABOVE Photographed in May 1916, this group of female clerks are from the Accounts Office at Swindon Works and were managed by Mr Kelynack, the Clerk in Charge. Mr Kelynack went on to become Chief Clerk to the CME in 1929. The back two rows reveal a very young group of girls who do not look much older than 15 or 16 years of age. For these female and girl clerks their position had a certain status attached to it. Although they were paid a lot less than male clerks, their roles were much admired and always had plenty of applicants. By 1918 the GWR was employing almost 3,000 female clerks across the network.

RIGHT This memo from STEAM's archive is from Mr Lockyer to Mr Kelynack, the Clerks in Charge who were mentioned in the previous two captions. The Government work required from Swindon Works was massive and the accounting for this was crucial. Mr Kelynack and his team of female clerks would have worked tirelessly to produce invoices and other accounts in relation to this.

Great Western Railway.

295

Locomotive, Carriage & Wagon Department,

ENGINEER'S OFFICE,

Swindon, Wilts,

Telegraphic Address,
CHURCHWARD, SWINDON.

Nat. Telephone Nº 32, SWINDON.

Enclosure

IN REPLY

TO YOUR:-

17th February, 191 5.

IN YOUR REPLY

W.

PLEASE QUOTE:-

Memo. to Mr. Kelynack.

Government work.

Please have the accompanying form completed as soon as possible to the 23rd January and let me have it again.

I wish to know each four weeks as soon as the information is available what the expenditure has been in connection with each job. The sheet will therefore be returned to you in due course and I shall be obliged if you will let me have it whenever the particulars for a further period have been entered.

I send herewith a supply of blank forms.

J. Lockyer

per

ABOVE Chief Ticket Inspector Lake sits in the centre of a large group of female ticket collectors in this image taken at Paddington station in 1916. It was only in the previous year that women were first employed as ticket collectors at stations on the GWR network. It brought about the same concerns that female clerks did in the offices, but it took the initiative of one Vera George to convince the company to employ women as ticket collectors. She wrote to the GWR in early 1915 asking to be employed as a ticket collector in order to free up men for more important work. The company adhered to the letter and Miss George went on to become the GWR's first female ticket collector.

RIGHT A lone female ticket collector stands inside an unidentified station punching a hole in the ticket she is checking. As the war progressed and more and more men went to fight, the range of jobs offered to women grew more varied and challenging. Many women relished the opportunities being offered to them and not only excelled in the new roles that they were undertaking, but also found it difficult to return to their former way of life once the war had ended and they had to relinquish the positions they held to the men returning home.

ABOVE A member of the Refreshment Department staff is photographed manning the platform trolley at Paddington station circa 1918. Photographs such as this, showing female workers employed in traditionally male roles, regularly appeared in the *GWR Magazine* during the war years. Whether this was a demonstration of pride or intrigue at women undertaking such work, it is difficult to judge.

RIGHT A dining car waitress in her crisp white apron stands in the doorway of dining car No 9545 on Platform 2 at Paddington station in 1917. Rail travel during the war was not just restricted to essential journeys; travel for pleasure continued, according to Mr Guy Calthrop, General Manager of the London & North Western Railway, who was asked to represent all of the railway companies before the Man Power Distribution Board. In his report of October 1916 he stated that 'there is an enormous amount of "joy-riding" on railways at the present time,' and facilities such as on-board dining for long journeys were as integral to the service the GWR offered its customers as they had been before the war began.

ABOVE These three porters at Didcot station had retired some years previous to this photograph being taken in 1917. However, due to men enlisting in the war some positions became vacant at the station and these men volunteered to fill them. The man in the centre of the image is David Ireland, and he is 73 years old. He joined the company in 1862 and in 1864 became a ticket collector at Didcot, until his retirement in 1910. The *GWR Magazine* reported in June 1917 that since his return to employment in December 1914 he had not been absent from duty for one day. The other men in the picture are James Stock, aged 68 (left), and George Wilkes, aged 66 (right).

RIGHT Engine driver Mr J. Lacey prepares for his last journey home from Paddington to Cardiff before he retired from the railways on 21 December 1916. Driver Lacey joined the South Wales Railway as a call boy in 1862 before working his way up through the ranks to become first a goods driver then eventually an express passenger engine driver based in Cardiff. From the age of 62 until his retirement at the age of 65, driver Lacey played his part in providing an essential train service during the early years of the war.

A.S.L.E & F. F.C. 1918.

ABOVE Many sports teams and clubs managed to continue during the war despite the shortage of men at home, as this photograph of the Swindon ASLEF (Associated Society of Locomotive Engineers & Firemen) Football Club taken in 1918 testifies. Being the ASLEF Club, it can be assumed that the men pictured were mainly locomotive drivers and firemen, men who remained at home to ensure that the railways in Britain continued to operate efficiently. The *GWR Magazine* kept its readers updated with the results and awards gained by the various sporting clubs formed under the umbrella of the company, and helped to ensure that some aspects of normality continued throughout the war years.

LEST WE FORGET

From the early days of the war efficient reporting structures and meticulous record-keeping ensured that as far as possible the fate of deceased soldiers was known. The GWR kept records of those of its men who lost their lives, and these reports were submitted to the Chief Officers Conference on a monthly basis. The monthly reports were subsequently assembled into a bound volume and we are fortunate to hold this unique and important record in the collection at STEAM. From these reports the *GWR Magazine* was able to publish tributes to the fallen, and the company produced Rolls of Honour and War Memorials to honour the dead.

There are some magnificent war memorials in Britain and one of the finest can be found at Paddington station dedicated to the men of the GWR who gave their lives fighting to protect their country. Made from bronze, granite and marble, and depicting a soldier reading a letter from home, it was installed in a prominent location on Platform 1 alongside the GWR Roll of Honour. Other memorials and Rolls of Honour were installed at stations and workshops across the GWR network. These varied in size and material ranging from the small wooden plaque from G Shop at Swindon Works, which listed the names of two employees, to the brass tablet remembering the 65 men from Nos 3, 15, 18 and 19d Shops who lost their lives.

As time goes on it is easy to lose sight of the original meaning and purpose of war memorials. In all, 25,479 Great Western men served in the First World War, and 2,524 of them never returned home. Unlike today's conflicts, those soldiers who lost their lives on battlefields overseas were buried where they fell; there was no repatriation of the bodies and no gravestone in a local cemetery where loved ones could go to pay their respects. This was a reality that would be inconceivable to us now, but during the First World War the loss of life was so great and the infrastructure and resources not in place to allow repatriation to take place.

The images included in this section are an illustration of the need that was felt throughout the country after the war to have a permanent way of honouring those men who went to fight and to remember their sacrifice.

RIGHT This poignant image of the GWR Roll of Honour on Platform 1 at Paddington station was taken on 11 November 1920, the second anniversary of the signing of the Armistice. As soon as the first reports of war casualties made their way back to the GWR in late 1914 the company began to compile a record of its men who lost their lives in the war. By the end of 1915 the first GWR Roll of Honour was placed at Paddington station. The list of those who died in service was regularly updated throughout the war and copies of the Roll of Honour placed at larger stations across the GWR network.

ABOVE On 11 November 1920 a large crowd of passengers and staff gathered around the Roll of Honour at Paddington to observe the 2-minute silence and witness the laying of wreaths in memory of the fallen. As had happened the previous year, all activity in the station was brought to a halt and trains that were scheduled to depart at 11.00am remained static during the 2-minute silence as a mark of respect.

RIGHT This official photograph of the GWR war memorial at Paddington station surrounded by flowers was taken following

its unveiling on 11 November 1922. The company recognised the need for a permanent tribute to its employees who lost their lives, so it commissioned this impressive monument to be installed in a prime location on Platform 1. Sculptor Charles Sargeant Jagger was given the task of designing the bronze figure of a soldier dressed in his greatcoat and helmet, reading a letter from home, while the granite and marble plinth and background were the work of Architect Thomas S. Tait. Installed in the plinth beneath the statue is a sealed casket containing a vellum roll on which the names of the fallen are inscribed.

ABOVE The GWR Chairman, the Rt Hon Viscount Churchill, is pictured here performing the unveiling of the War Memorial at Paddington. The unveiling ceremony was introduced by the Vicar and Rural Dean of Paddington and, following the singing of a hymn, Viscount Churchill performed his duty, accompanied by the Archbishop of Canterbury and various GWR officials. Approximately 6,000 people, the majority bereaved relatives and grieving colleagues, attended the ceremony. To safely accommodate such a crowd and to ensure people got a good view of the event, staging was constructed on Platforms 2 and 3, and infilled with further staging built upon carriage trucks placed on the track between Platforms 1 and 2. Such was the strength of feeling throughout the country at wanting to honour its war dead that the GWR was prepared to go to extraordinary lengths to pay tribute to its lost employees.

RIGHT This booklet from the collection at STEAM gives a detailed account of the unveiling ceremony of the Paddington war memorial in 1922. It was produced in January 1923 and was included, together with an accompanying photograph of the memorial, in the *GWR Magazine*.

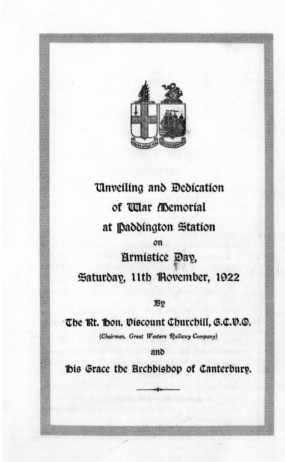

ABOVE Here we see the unveiling of the brass war memorial tablets for Nos 3, 15, 18 and 19d Shops in the Carriage & Wagon Works at Swindon on 20 October 1923. The unveiling was performed by Mr E. T. J. Evans, Manager of the Carriage & Wagon Works, accompanied by the Mayor of Swindon, Mr A. Harding. Up to 2,000 employees and relatives attended the ceremony, with, one can assume by the number of women in the image, the widows of those being honoured given a prominent place at the front of the crowd.

Unveiling and Dedication
of War Memorial
at Paddington Station
on
Armistice Day,
Saturday, 11th November, 1922

By

The Rt. Hon. Viscount Churchill, G.C.V.O.
(Chairman, Great Western Railway Company)

and

His Grace the Archbishop of Canterbury.

THE
SECOND
WORLD
WAR

SWINDON WORKS AND
THE SECOND WORLD WAR

The photographs in this chapter not only highlight the work that was undertaken at Swindon Works during the Second World War, but also act as a visual comparison to the work that had taken place there during the First World War.

It was only a short period of 21 years since Swindon Works had last been on hand to help fulfil orders for the Government and the war effort. In the interwar period the company had faced a lot of uncertainty; the General Strike of 1926 and the onset of the Great Depression in the early 1930s had caused financial difficulties for the GWR. However, under the direction of its Chief Mechanical Engineer, C. B. Collett, Swindon Works was continuing to build locomotives. In the 1920s two of the most iconic classes of express locomotive were built, the 'Castles' and the 'Kings', and by 1937 the output of locomotives, carriages and wagons was at its peak for a number of years.

It is not surprising that when war broke out in September 1939 Collett was reluctant to undertake munitions work. In the First World War it had taken precedence over the normal railway work, which was considered equally as important by the company. Despite the reluctance to participate, the orders for munitions and special vehicles soon came into the Works. As with the First World War, some of the first orders were for the supply of ambulance trains. This was quickly followed by the overhaul of the 'Dean Goods' locomotives, then a period of munitions work between late 1940 and 1943. Much of the war work that was undertaken at the Works was shrouded in secrecy and there is a surprising lack of written records documenting it. However, the photographic record is exemplary and provides a comprehensive account of the work carried out not only in Swindon, but also by the GWR as a whole. Wartime photograph albums show an array of work including the production of guns, bombs, shells, tanks, landing craft, cranes, bridges and sundry items.

In 1941 Collett retired and the post of CME was given to F. W. Hawksworth, who saw Swindon Works through to the end of the war. By early 1945, after almost five years of wartime pressures and shortages, the Works was on its knees, and when victory was declared in Europe in May of that year it could not have come soon enough for the Great Western Railway. The challenge facing Hawksworth now was the rebuilding of the Works to its pre-war standard.

LEFT Some rather intricate hot work is taking place in this photograph taken in K Shop, the Coppersmiths, in November 1940. The men are welding exploder containers for 250lb bombs that had been ordered by the Ministry of Aircraft Production. Airborne attacks during the war were extensive and hugely damaging, and Swindon Works helped to fulfil the requirements for bombs of a number of different sizes used by the Royal Air Force and the Allied forces.

BELOW Completed 250lb bombs are loaded onto GWR open wagon No 44 in December 1940. As with the majority of the war work undertaken at the Works, specialist equipment was built to cater for this new and unusual work. Here we can see a special lifting mechanism that was used to carry eight 250lb bombs at a time; this allowed for faster loading times and only required two men to operate it.

RIGHT A step up in bomb size here, this time to the 1,000lb bomb. This image, taken in March 1941, shows two 1,000lb bombs sitting next to each other in X Shop, one with a fin and one without. The 1,000lb bomb was generally used on industrial targets and was carried by the RAF on many aircraft, including the Hawker Typhoon. Apart from the 2,000lb and 4,000lb bombs, this was the largest of the standard bombs used by the RAF, with almost 1 million being made nationally during the war years.

ABOVE More than 2,000 bodies for the 4,000lb bombs were constructed at Swindon Works. This image, taken in L2 Tank Shop in December 1940, shows the construction of these bodies prior to being sent to the Royal Arsenal at Woolwich for filling. These were the largest bombs ever to be built at the Works during both wars and were designed to be carried by the RAF's heavy bombers. In total, 60,000 bombs of all sizes were supplied by Swindon Works.

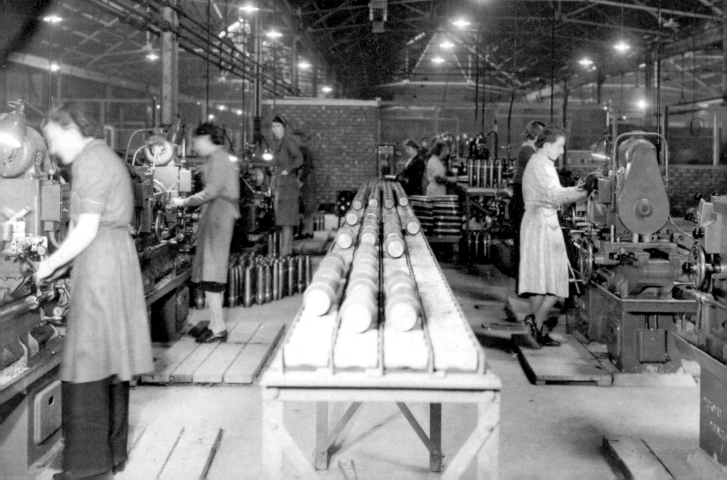

TOP LEFT This photograph, taken in September 1941, shows the alterations taking place in 24F Shop to accommodate the new shell production for the Ministry of Supply. In most instances the new production lines were squeezed into existing workshops at Swindon and normal work carried on. 24 Shop, on the Carriage & Wagon side of the Works, was fitted out with two production lines for 25-pounder shells. The refurbishment was quite a feat and required the excavation of new foundations for heavy machinery and furnaces.

BOTTOM LEFT The production line mentioned in the previous caption is in full operation in this photograph of 24F Shop from February 1942. The various machines are fully manned by female operatives, who finished, turned, weighed and riveted

the 25-pounder shells and in total produced more than 63,000 of them. A stack of machined shells can be seen on the floor to the left and centre of the image.

ABOVE This photograph of the shell production line in 24F Shop provides a much wider view of the workshop space for shell inspection. Thousands of shells are stacked against the brick walls ready to be dealt with, and more are lined up on the workbenches. In this image the women are working side by side with their male counterparts. Three men can be seen in this photograph, with the women outnumbering the men by at least five to one. The man in the centre of the image wearing a shirt and tie and a white apron is probably the foreman.

LEFT In March 1942 four women are operating a large pressing machine in Q Shop. They are making 4.5-inch copper bands for ammunition shells, which can be seen fully manufactured in the following image. The women are all wearing overalls with their hair tied back, but there is a distinct lack of safety equipment, such as goggles or gloves. Note also that the windows have been blacked out as part of Swindon Works' air raid precautions.

TOP RIGHT These women have been tasked with the pressing on of copper bands and insertion of base plates for 25-pounder quick-firing, high-explosive, streamline shells. They are using a specialist Aldous-Campbell Ltd high-pressure machine that fits both copper band and base plate securely in position. The lady to the right of the machine is holding a shell in position, and a notice board (just out of shot) states that two presses, one of 8 seconds and another of 5 seconds, are required by the machine to seal the shell.

BOTTOM RIGHT By 1943 the majority of Allied munitions production was undertaken by America and Canada. This eased the pressure on British workshops, as there had become a serious shortage of materials. This image of 24F Shop in February 1942 shows one of the shell production lines being packed up, ready to be shipped to America. These particular boxes are marked up for New York, a city that alone housed more than 300 war plants and factories during the Second World War.

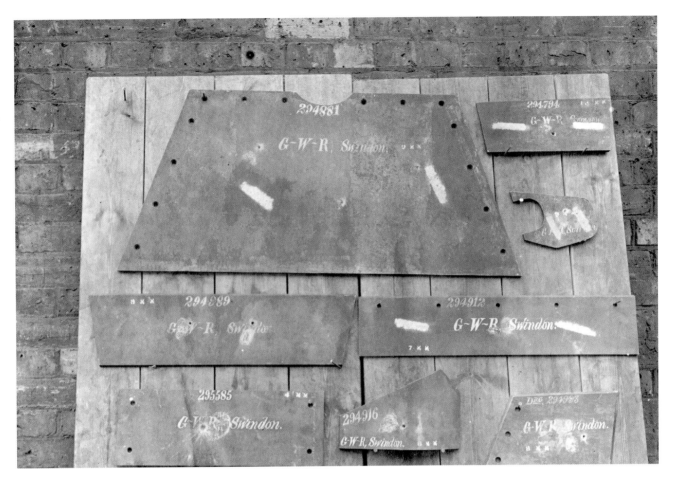

TOP LEFT This side view of a 2-pounder 'pom-pom' gun mounting built for the Admiralty at Swindon Works was taken in AM Shop in February 1943 and shows the ammunition positioned in the side trays. The barrels and breaches were already supplied, but Swindon carried out the swivel and elevating gear manufacture on this particular quick-firing gun. Swindon was also responsible for the manufacture of mountings and shields for Hotchkiss guns, 6-pounder guns and 13.5-inch hyper-velocity guns, as well as parts for Bofors, 3.7-inch AA and 25-pounder guns.

BOTTOM LEFT This anti-aircraft 6-pounder naval gun was manufactured for the Admiralty in W Shop at Swindon Works. It comes with a mounting that would have allowed it to be fixed to the ground, a building roof or a small ship, and a shield to protect the gunner. Although this gun is small in size,

use of most anti-aircraft guns required weeks of intensive training, particularly if you joined an anti-aircraft regiment. Although the anti-aircraft guns that were positioned on the home front coastal defences were not particularly effective, they did shoot down a number of German V1 flying bombs ('doodlebugs') during their time in operation.

ABOVE In addition to the munitions and specialist vehicles built at Swindon, the Works also undertook some more unusual tasks for the Government. This photograph, taken in May 1941, shows some bullet-proof steel cut in the Works that has undergone firing tests to determine suitability. The steel has varying sizes of thickness, and the bullet holes and markings are clearly visible. The process of hardening the steel was carried out in V (Boiler) Shop.

TOP LEFT One of the earliest tasks contracted to the GWR by the Ministry of Supply was the erection of tanks for supply overseas. Thousands of tank components were being made by all the British railway companies during the initial years of the war, and this image of A Erecting Shop at Swindon Works, taken in June 1941, shows some of those components being brought together to form the body of 25-27-ton tanks. The tanks under construction are Infantry Tank Mark II, or Matilda II as they were commonly known. They were difficult and complex tanks to build and required a skilled workforce with specialist machinery to correctly manufacture the model.

BOTTOM LEFT Some three months later, in September 1941, three Matilda II tanks were photographed leaving A Erecting Shop on Rectank wagons. The tanks are incomplete and are presumably ready to be transported elsewhere for final assembly. These are just three of nearly 3,000 such tanks produced by heavy manufacturing companies throughout

Britain between 1939 and 1943. They were heavily armoured vehicles used by the British Infantry, most prominently in the North Africa Campaign, where their success earned them the nickname 'Queen of the Desert'.

ABOVE In August 1941 the GWR began building the first of a large number of motor landing craft in the Carriage & Wagon shops at Swindon. No 13 Wagon Frame Shop was where this work took place, and in this image one of the first batch of 12 landing craft can be seen under construction in February 1942. The bulkheads and frames are shown erected on a jig, while the hull bottom strakes are in the process of being fitted. Bullet-proof cladding, the engines, propellers and other fittings would then have been added and the craft made ready for launch in May 1942. At 40 feet in length and with a 13ft 6in beam, these craft were too wide to be moved by rail so had to be transported to the coast at Southampton by a tractor-drawn road vehicle.

ABOVE The motor landing craft were made in readiness for the invasion of Europe, their primary purpose being to ferry troops from transport ships onto occupied shores. This image of Motor Landing Craft (MLC) No 153 shows the flat-bottom construction that enabled the craft to run up onto a beach, and the lowerable ramp from which the troops could swiftly disembark. These GWR-built landing crafts, and many variations built by other manufacturing companies, were used during the Second World War for amphibious assaults on enemy-occupied Europe, starting with the invasion of Sicily in June 1943 through to the D-Day invasion of Normandy in June 1944.

RIGHT Also built in the Carriage & Wagon Works at Swindon were 50 of these midget submarine superstructures, which were produced for the Admiralty. The superstructure was made of mahogany and covered in outer curtains that protected the driver and his assistant from the flow of water when submerged. All joints had to be precision-made in order to prevent any water penetration into the submarine, and the vessel was built to withstand water pressure of 90lb to the square inch, so allowing it to submerge to a considerable depth. The work on the midget submarines was top secret – only the men directly involved in their design and construction knew about them and they were sworn to secrecy. The screens surrounding the submarine in this image are testament to the sensitive nature of much of the war work carried out at Swindon Works.

BELOW This official image taken in April 1942 shows timber components for Bailey bridges being manufactured in No 2 Shop, the Sawmill, at Swindon Works. In the book *It Can Now Be Revealed* it is documented that the GWR 'made 27,157 timber components and 13,700 packing timbers as well as other parts' for Bailey bridges. The Bailey bridge was developed by Donald Bailey, who worked for the British War Office; it was a portable, prefabricated structure that was used extensively during the war and was strong enough to carry even a tank. As this image shows, the parts for a Bailey bridge were simple, but they had to be precisely manufactured in order to fit together correctly; an essential test for the manufacturers, including Swindon Works, was to assemble a bridge in the workshops to ensure this was the case.

THE GREAT WESTERN UNDER ATTACK

Throughout the Second World War Britain was faced with a barrage of air attacks from the German Luftwaffe. From September 1940 until May 1941 the Germans carried out a series of relentless air raids that became known as the Blitz, which affected the major cities and towns in Britain, as well as the important ports on the coast, but it was London that bore the brunt of the attacks. The GWR's network, which stretched from London to the South West, through to the Midlands, South Wales and the North West, suddenly became caught up in this horrific scenario. The photographs in this chapter capture the devastation that the GWR experienced during the war, but they also illustrate the strong determination shown by the company and its employees to combat the effects of the air raids and to protect themselves from attacks.

The GWR's principal terminus, Paddington, was at the heart of the capital and was subjected to a number of attacks during the Blitz. The company's head office, also based at Paddington, was evacuated from the city and relocated to Aldermaston in Berkshire in an attempt to keep the administrative side of the railway running efficiently. Despite extensive bomb damage to stations, factories, permanent way, locomotives and rolling stock, the GWR continued to operate as normal where possible. In October 1940 the *GWR Magazine* reported that the company's repair staff were 'prepared at all costs to do whatever may be necessary to make good any damage that has been caused'. Adolf Hitler may have used the Blitz as an attempt to destroy British morale, but what was actually born out of the rubble and ruins was an indomitable spirit of a nation under attack. This wartime spirit was adopted by the GWR and other railway companies and kept the railways running.

During the war the aim of the GWR was not only to keep its network operating, but also to protect its property, assets, staff and passengers. Air raid precautions were put in place at most of the major stations and depots, which included sandbag protection, specially built air raid shelters, blacked-out windows and the use of gas masks. Perhaps the most important aspect of air raid precaution and response was the use of specially trained employees, who, under the auspices of the Home Guard, fire marshals and ARP wardens, protected Great Western property with fearless heroism.

ABOVE This busy office scene, pictured in 1940, was part of the GWR's Emergency Headquarters located at Aldermaston, Berkshire. Twelve departments were evacuated from the head office at Paddington at the start of the war and relocated to this purpose-built site, comprising six separate buildings. Special trains conveyed clerical staff from their homes to the station at Aldermaston each day, and other country houses on the outskirts of London were also used to accommodate head office workers.

ABOVE Railway stations were on high alert during the war years. The principal stations on the GWR network were used by hundreds of people each day and a direct bomb strike on any of these stations could potentially cause multiple fatalities. Air raid precautions were put in place to minimise the effect of bomb damage, and this image of Birmingham Snow Hill station shows the use of sandbags to protect buildings, and their occupants, from fire and shrapnel damage.

LEFT This rather intriguing photo of West Ealing Goods Yard was taken in 1940, and the strange molehill-shaped mounds dotted along the track are air raid shelters that could be accessed quickly by the goods staff should an attack be imminent. The pipes sticking from the top of the shelters were probably used for ventilation purposes or as chimneys for stoves and heaters.

RIGHT An anti-aircraft platform can be seen in this image of Swindon station, but what is most intriguing is the very small Swindon Junction sign hanging in the centre of the platform canopy in front of the Turog advertisement. In 1940 precautions were put in place to thwart possible German parachute invaders. For the GWR this meant the removal of station signs, but nationally it included the removal of signposts, milestones and AA village signs. The idea was to confuse foreign invaders should they land in the country. This small sign was a means of allowing general passengers a discreet way of identifying where they were.

LEFT This notice was issued to passengers in August 1940 by the GWR's General Manager, James Milne. The safety of staff and passengers was of the utmost importance and the GWR was obliged to issue the correct directives. Many of the GWR's principal stations had huge overall roofs built from glass, iron, steel and wood, and the threat of these huge structures collapsing during a bombing raid was extremely high.

GREAT WESTERN RAILWAY

Notice to Passengers

Passengers are advised to take shelter during an Air Raid and not to remain on the station platforms, where there may be a serious risk of danger from falling glass and splinters.

J. MILNE,

August, 1940.   General Manager.

TOP LEFT Bomb damage to stations was inevitable after the sustained air attacks by the German Luftwaffe in late 1940 and early 1941. This photograph shows the damage to the station at Royal Oak, just outside Paddington. The two carriages of a London to Swansea train show the effect of a blast, including fire damage and broken windows. The track, platform and station buildings have also suffered from the blast, with twisted rails and broken slabs evident in the centre of the image.

BOTTOM LEFT This is the departure side of Paddington station following the explosion of a parachute mine on 17 April 1941. A gaping hole can be seen to the right of the image where the station offices were located, and a clean-up operation is well under way. The explosion claimed the lives of 18 people, including six staff, with a further 97 people injured. It also destroyed No 2 Booking Hall, which was situated adjacent to Platform 1.

ABOVE Another view of Paddington following the explosion of the parachute mine, this time showing the internal damage to the station, particularly to Platform 1. Despite the clear-up operation taking place, passengers are still gathered on the platform awaiting the arrival of the next train. The efficient engineering capabilities of the GWR meant that the company was able to resume normal service as quickly as possible.

ABOVE Fire-fighting by the GWR was as important in the Second World War as it had been in the First. Incendiary bombs (designed to start fires) were used extensively during the war and caused devastation across many of the country's cities and towns. By October 1943 the GWR had in operation 250 petrol trailer fire pumps, as seen in this image from July 1940. They were located at stations, goods yards, docks and factories, and this example is being hauled by an ex-GWR Express Cartage van, which was salvaged from the scrap heap in order to carry out fire-fighting duties.

TOP RIGHT This image shows members of the GWR fire brigade at Paddington station taking part in a drill. Training was an important part of fire-fighting and kept employees prepared in case of an emergency. The enthusiasm for drill work was so

great that in January 1943 a competition was introduced. The inaugural all-line trailer pump competition took place at Paddington Mint Stables and comprised 13 male teams and four female teams, with Exeter Locomotive Depot and Cardiff Queen Street station winning respectively. The competitions continued until the end of the war.

BOTTOM RIGHT This Dennis fire engine was purchased by the Swindon Works fire brigade in December 1942 and was used to strengthen its wartime capabilities. The older Dennis fire engine, pictured earlier in this book, stood down as 'first call' but continued to remain in service. The new fire engine could accommodate six or seven men and contained 2,000 feet of hose. It was also painted battleship grey so it was not easily spotted in an air raid.

RIGHT During an air raid the threat of poison gas bombs being dropped by the German Luftwaffe was extremely high. Mustard gas was the most deadly gas available and could take up to 12 hours to take effect, so 38 million gas masks were distributed in Britain to protect against any ill effects should gas bombs be dropped. After an air raid GWR staff would continue their normal duties, but in some instances would continue to wear their gas masks. This image shows a porter at Paddington station wearing his mask. It must have been difficult to carry out normal tasks with limited visibility and restricted movement.

LEFT A GWR commercial van has been converted into an emergency ambulance in this image from May 1940. Following air raid precautions, the driver and messenger are wearing gas masks and tin helmets, while the ambulance has been fitted with a headlamp blackout cover. Night-time driving was dangerous during the blackout, so many vehicles had their wings and sides painted white to add some reflection and improve their visibility.

ABOVE Blackouts were challenging times for some GWR employees, as this image of a shunter taken at Bristol shows. Limited lighting during an air raid posed a serious health & safety risk, especially in busy depots or marshalling yards. Even in daylight the task of coupling and uncoupling wagons was a dangerous job, but at night it was even worse, and during a blackout it must have been a daunting experience, even for a skilled shunter. Shunters were required to use lamps that had shades attached, which meant they were less visible to aircraft during an air raid, but it also had a negative impact on their working visibility.

ABOVE A signalman in his gas mask continues normal duties at this unknown signal box. But what is interesting about this photograph is the strange-looking metal cabinet with its door ajar standing in the corner of the signal box – it is actually a small air raid shelter for the signalman to retreat to. The shelters were nicknamed 'coffins' as there was just enough space to fit one person. The large number of windows in a signal box made them dangerous places to be in an air raid, so the 'coffins' were installed to provide shelter from shattering glass and debris. They were made of boiler-plate and were manufactured in the L2 (Tank) Shop at Swindon Works.

LEFT This publicity shot of a driver in his gas mask and tin helmet on the footplate of 'Castle' Class locomotive *Evesham Abbey* was taken in August 1940. Drivers were requested to wear the masks periodically so they got accustomed to them should an air raid take place. It has already been mentioned that the wearing of masks would have reduced visibility for other GWR employees, but for drivers and firemen it must have been particularly awkward, and very hot.

ABOVE A train speeding through the countryside at night was a prime target for the German Luftwaffe; the glow from the locomotive firebox and light from the carriages made a train all too visible to the enemy. One of the blackout measures introduced by the GWR was the anti-glare screen. This image of 'Castle' Class locomotive *Highclere Castle* shows an anti-glare screen attached to the cab roof and tender. During daylight the screen could be rolled back and, should an air raid be called, it could be quickly pulled back over the cab. This screen only covered the roof of the cab, but some screens covered the sides too.

RIGHT This photograph of 'Saint' Class locomotive *Madresfield Court* shows damage to the cab after it came under aircraft machine gun fire at Yarnbrook, near Westbury. Even though precautionary measures were put in place, some locomotives still came under fire. During the war drivers and firemen reported that some of the German fighter planes flew so close to their trains that they could see the swastika on the tail, and even a waving pilot. Quite often a German fighter plane would chase a train for miles, only to fly off and disappear into the clouds. It must have been a scary moment for those on board.

BELOW This image was taken on 30 April 1941, the morning after an air raid at Keyham station, Plymouth, and shows extensive damage to 'Hall' Class locomotive *Bowden Hall* after a bomb landed just feet away from the right-hand side of the cab. The driver and fireman had a lucky escape as they had been sheltering under the steps of the signal box when the bomb was dropped. Their entire cab was destroyed, and the signal box also suffered significant damage, with all but a few windows smashed in the explosion.

ABOVE On 20 August 1940 Newton Abbot station was attacked by three German planes, and these two images show the devastation that was caused by both bomb damage and extensive machine gun fire. Parts of the station were completely destroyed, together with damage to 15 locomotives, 52 passenger carriages and 22 goods wagons. In total, 60 people died or were seriously injured. The first picture shows pannier tank No 2785 attached by chain to 'Grange' Class locomotive No 6801 *Aylburton Grange* to stop it falling into a bomb crater!

ABOVE A '4300' Class 'Mogul' locomotive, No 8314, lies amongst the debris following an air raid in Weymouth on 17 January 1941. 'Star' Class locomotive *Princess Charlotte* can be seen to the right of the photograph and has escaped the worst of the damage. The South Coast of Britain was easy prey for the German Luftwaffe based in northern France, and the ports of Weymouth and Portland were prime targets for bombers due to their naval connections.

LEFT A rather forlorn-looking carriage can be seen here at the entrance to No 2 Tunnel at Foxes Wood near Bristol in 1941. A bomb had hit the tunnel mouth and ricocheted into the carriage, completely destroying it. The initial damage to the tunnel can be seen at the top of the entrance portal, but the coach took the brunt of the explosion. The whole side of the coach has fallen away revealing the vulnerability of such vehicles in these extreme circumstances.

ABOVE Swindon Works should have been a prime target for the German Luftwaffe, but it remained relatively unscathed by any air raids on the town. This image, taken on 27 July 1942, shows a bomb crater on the edge of No 24 Shop in the Carriage & Wagon Works. This was not a direct hit, but the damaged roof and shattered windows of No 24 Shop illustrate the force of such a bomb explosion. Several workmen are examining the crater, probably thankful the bomb did not land any closer.

LEFT In another view of the Works following the air raid on 27 July 1942, the gas holder at the gas works is pockmarked by machine gun fire from a lone aircraft that had swooped over the town early in the morning. A fire broke out in the gas holder, but it was quickly put out and the holes were plugged with clay to prevent any further damage. It is interesting to note the strange breathing apparatus worn by the two men on the left – presumably masks to combat the effects of any escaping gas.

ABOVE This image, taken on Saturday 31 July 1943 (August Bank Holiday), shows hoards of passengers at Paddington station. In 1939 the slogan 'Is Your Journey Really Necessary?' was introduced to discourage people from travelling within Britain, and was used to remind people to save fuel and allow trains to transport soldiers and war supplies instead. By the summer of 1943 these regulations had been relaxed slightly, which encouraged more pleasure travel. On this day, 34,000 passengers were dispatched from Paddington, with 40,000 recorded the day before. All the trains to the West Country were loaded to capacity and some passengers were left behind!

ABOVE In another busy view of Paddington station on August Bank Holiday 1943, the scene looks relatively dark, with only a few beams of sunlight coming through the roof, much of the glass roof having been blacked out for air raid precautions. The carriage standing at Platform 4 is also unusually dark. In a circular from 20 April 1942 the GWR noted that there was a shortage of constituents for making cream paint, and the new directive was to paint all carriages brown. The chocolate and cream livery for which the GWR was famed was gradually phased out during the war period and only special coaches, such as saloons, Riviera stock and diesel railcars continued to be painted in the two colours.

ABOVE The Local Defence Volunteers (LDV) organisation was formed in May 1940, but in August it changed its name to the Home Guard. More than 1 million men joined, their purpose being to defend British shores against invasion from Germany. The GWR saw the need to protect its own property during the war and formed its own official Home Guard battalions and platoons. This image from July 1943 shows one of the GWR's Home Guard battalions on parade at Castle Bar Park in London.

TOP RIGHT This photograph shows the presentation of an award to Home Guard member Mr C. Wheeler in April 1944. He was a member of the 13th Battalion of the Wiltshire Home Guard, which was formed in 1943 to protect GWR property in Swindon and was made up entirely of GWR employees. The men of this battalion maintained their jobs with the company in the day and trained with the Home Guard in the evenings.

BOTTOM RIGHT Another group shot of the 13th Battalion was this time taken at a rifle shoot on the chalk ridge at Liddington, near Swindon. The Home Guard evolved to be a well-equipped and trained army and would partake in numerous drills and training exercises such as that illustrated here. Not only were they ready for invasion but they could also perform bomb disposal and man anti-aircraft artillery. This was a far cry from the comedic image portrayed by the popular television series *Dad's Army*.

ABOVE Swindon Works was considered a prime target for aircraft strikes during the Second World War. Here, two members of the Home Guard are manning an anti-aircraft gun platform on the roof of uniform supplier Compton Sons & Webb at the Works. This was one of a number of anti-aircraft platforms erected around the site. The Home Guard was well trained to man these types of weapon and its members could be called away from their normal day jobs should an air raid warning be issued.

ABOVE By the end of 1944 the threat of invasion from Germany became unlikely and it was decided that the Home Guard could be stood down. This image, taken on 3 December 1944, shows the stand-down parade of the 13th Battalion at Swindon Works. The Home Guard was fully disbanded on 31 December 1945.

AND STILL THE
RAILWAYS CARRY ON

In this chapter we look at the operational role that the GWR played in the war effort through a collection of images that show the movement of troops and equipment, the supply of engines and rolling stock, and the work of the company's docks and shipping services. This is an area for which there is a wealth of photographic material at STEAM due to the fact that, where possible, the GWR took official images of the war work that the company undertook.

As the outbreak of war looked increasingly likely in the months leading up to September 1939, plans were being put in place to prepare the country for the inevitable conflict. The railways were an integral part of these plans and the GWR was itself making preparations for air raid precautions, the stockpiling of supplies and altered passenger timetables. As soon as war was declared the railway's plans were put into action and the evacuation of children from the cities and the movement of troops, equipment and supplies began.

The request for locomotives for use overseas was met with the supply of 108 'Dean Goods' engines from GWR stock. The company also fulfilled orders for the supply of ambulance trains, rolling stock and other specialist vehicles, which are illustrated in this chapter. The entry of America into the war in late 1941 added another dimension to the work that the GWR undertook. One very special top secret order was for the supply of the 'Alive' train for use by General Eisenhower during his visits to Britain and latterly occupied Europe. Very few details exist of this train, but we are fortunate to have a photograph of one of the Alive Train carriages in the collection at STEAM.

With Britain being the US's main entry point into Europe, troops, equipment and even locomotives were shipped over from America to the GWR's South Wales docks. The company docks were also the entry and exit routes for British Expeditionary Forces and military equipment, so were strategically important and very busy places during the Second World War. The GWR's ships, docks and railways also played a vital operational role in wartime missions such as the famous evacuation of Dunkirk, D-Day and the evacuation of London during the flying bomb campaign.

ABOVE One of the very first wartime roles in which the GWR was engaged was the evacuation of children from cities to the relative safety of the countryside. Even before war was declared, plans were drawn up for evacuation so the GWR and the other major railway companies were prepared and on standby to put these plans into action. On 31 August 1939, the day before Germany invaded Poland, the order to begin the evacuation was given. The very next day the mass movement of children began and continued until 4 September. The GWR was responsible for the majority of the children moved from north and east London and, while most of the evacuation trains departed from Ealing Broadway, this image shows groups of children being off-loaded from a double-decker bus outside the Departure Platform at Paddington station during the four days of evacuation in September 1939.

ABOVE This moving image of evacuees making their way along Platform 4 at Paddington was also taken during the four-day evacuation of London and other major cities in September 1939. On 1 September 58 evacuation trains were run by the GWR alone, carrying 44,042 children from the capital to the countryside. By 4 September the number was reduced to 28 trains transporting 17,796 children. In total the GWR ran 163 trains from London during this four-day period, evacuating 112,994 children. The evacuation story did not end there, however, for the GWR was subsequently involved with the re-evacuation of children from the south and east coasts to safer places, and the evacuation of more children from the London area.

TOP RIGHT Paper salvage was introduced by the Government at the outbreak of war in 1939, designed to encourage the recycling of materials to aid the war effort. Paper salvage became compulsory in late 1940 and fines were put in place for companies and authorities that failed to sort their waste. This image from December 1941 shows a wastepaper van collecting a large amount of paper from the General Stores at Swindon Works.

BOTTOM RIGHT Another view from December 1941, this time of a paper recycling cart outside the General Stores at Swindon Works. Bound bundles of paperwork and ledgers can be seen piled on the cart ready to be taken away to be pulped. Although the operation was a worthwhile effort, it is quite sad to see the paperwork being destroyed – historians studying the GWR are now plagued by gaps in the historical records. By 1945 the GWR had sent thousands of tons of waste to paper mills.

LEFT As well as paper, the GWR was also committed to salvaging other material. In August 1940 the General Manager, James Milne, invited employees to join the GWR Salvage Corps. This leaflet was issued to encourage staff to salvage a whole host of items including metals, timber, glass, rubber, bones and foodstuffs. A quote from inside the leaflet reads 'Salvage feeds the guns that fight the Huns' – a reference to the German enemy.

BELOW This special salvage van was converted from an Iron Mink wagon. It was used to collect scrap from principal stations on the GWR's network and deliver it to a number of the company's Stores Department depots for resorting. The van was fitted out with four separate bins for specific types of material and was coloured bright blue with bright white lettering.

ABOVE In a cruel twist of fate, this image from 15 November 1940 shows bomb damage to the GWR's salvage warehouse at Park Royal in north-west London. From 7 September 1940 London was bombed for 57 consecutive days and nights, destroying about a third of the city. This particular area of London, with its high concentration of industrial activity, was a prime target for the Germans.

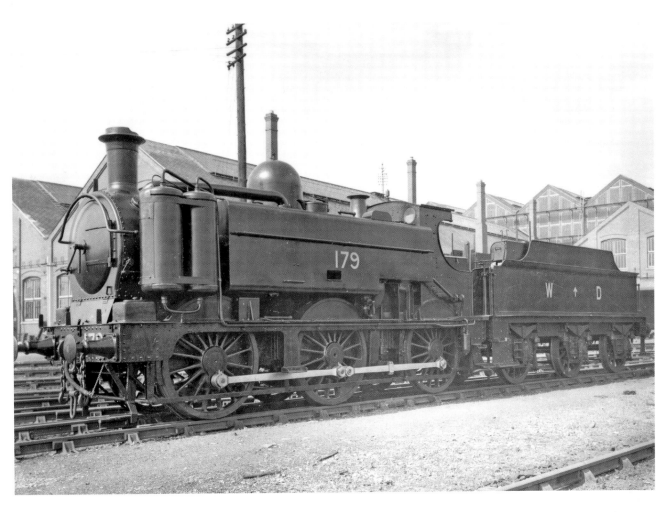

TOP LEFT 'Dean Goods' 0-6-0 tender locomotive No 2430 is pictured here in its wartime livery. The tender is painted with 'WD' for War Department and the engine bears its War Department number, 177. In late 1939 and again in late 1940 the GWR was called upon to supply a total of 108 'Dean Goods' locomotives for service overseas. This lightweight but strong class was regarded as ideal for war work so the locomotives were quickly got ready; a number had to be reinstated and overhauled, having been withdrawn from service prior to the war. It is interesting to note that No 2430 was one of a number of 'Dean Goods' locomotives that had already seen overseas service in the First World War.

BOTTOM LEFT This official photograph of 'Dean Goods' locomotive No 2533 was taken at Swindon Works in October 1939 prior to its shipment overseas. Again, the locomotive bears its War Department black livery and new engine

number, and would have also been fitted with Westinghouse brakes as part of its preparation for war service. Seventy-nine 'Dean Goods' were shipped to France, and during the invasion of that country by Germany in 1940 there were heavy losses of these locomotives as a number were destroyed during fighting and the remainder fell under the control of German forces, who operated them for their own use while in control of the country.

ABOVE In another official photograph of a 'Dean Goods' locomotive made ready for war service, we see No 179, which was one of ten of the class fitted with pannier tanks and condensing equipment. The addition of the pannier tank, used together with the tender, meant that these modified locomotives had a much longer operational capacity, particularly useful when working in hot countries, while the attached condensing tanks reduced water consumption even further.

TOP LEFT War Department 2-8-0 locomotives are under construction in AE Shop at Swindon Works in May 1943. In order to meet the demand for locomotives for war work, in 1942 the War Department placed an order with the GWR to build 80 LMS Stanier Class 8F 2-8-0 freight locomotives, for use both at home and overseas. The short supply of raw materials meant that the building of these locomotives took longer than expected, and this image shows a number of the first batch of 27 engines under construction, more than a year after the first order was placed.

BOTTOM LEFT Great Western tender No W84 is featured in this official image taken in April 1941. Formerly No 2641, this 4,000-gallon engine tender was requisitioned by the Government for use with a fire-fighting train. Such trains were located at key points across the network to react quickly in the event of an air raid. The water in the tenders was used to put out fires, and one of the fire-fighting trains had six tenders attached, which held up to 15,000 gallons of water, enough to supply water to attached petrol motor pumps for up to 2½ hours.

ABOVE This sorry sight of four 0-6-0 'Dean Goods' locomotives in the process of being scrapped dates from the late 1940s. Identified as Nos 2479, 2576, 2425 and 2399, all built during the 1890s, these locomotives would have seen service in both World Wars. With many 'Dean Goods' having been rescued from the scrap heap in 1939 and 1940 due to them being needed for war service, it was inevitable that once locomotive building resumed in earnest after the war many of these older engines were destined for the scrap heap once again.

2nd Coach.   5th Coach.   6th Coach.   3rd Coach.

ABOVE These two disturbing photographs (above and right) tell of the terrible consequences of the effect of war on ordinary civilians. On the night of 4 November 1940 locomotive No 6028 *King George VI* left Paddington station hauling 13 coaches heading for Penzance. As the train was nearing Norton Fitzwarren in Somerset it was switched from the main line to a relief line to allow a newspaper train to pass by. Due to a misreading of signals, exacerbated by blackout conditions, the driver of the passenger train did not realise that he had been diverted to a relief line and began to accelerate in order to make up for time lost previously in the journey. He realised his mistake when the newspaper train overtook him on the main line to the right and immediately shut the regulator and applied the brake. But it was too late and the packed train, carrying 900 passengers, became derailed at the catch points at the end of the relief line.

BELOW Twenty-seven people were killed in the crash, including the fireman, and 56 passengers were injured. The driver, incredibly, survived. The engine and the first seven coaches were derailed, while the last six amazingly stayed upright. This image shows soldiers from the Royal Pioneer Corps, who carried out the rescue work and helped to clear the wreckage. These two photographs of the Norton Fitzwarren train crash are part of a set of images contained in a workbook detailing the technical details of this awful accident. The workbook was compiled by Mr Alexander Christison who at the time was a Divisional Locomotive Superintendent based at Newton Abbot. An investigation following the accident found that the derailment was caused by driver error. However, it was also accepted that blame could also be attributed to the blackout conditions in which he was operating, and the strain he was under caused by the fact that the night before his house in Acton had been destroyed by bombing during the Blitz.

ABOVE This official photograph of an ambulance train car was taken on behalf of the Swindon Works Drawing Office in October 1939. It is one of 16 LMS 57-foot Corridor 3rd Class coaches that were converted at Swindon during late 1939 for use in ambulance trains both at home and overseas. Car No 6204, seen here, was converted into an administrative car that formed part of an ambulance train for use on Britain's railways.

The administrative car was comprehensively fitted out with a sick officers compartment, kit store, pharmacy compartment, office and medical store. The exterior of the car was painted khaki with a white and red cross in the centre of the body on each side, and it is interesting to note that blackout precautions were taken into account during the conversion of the vehicles, with all the external windows of the carriage painted black.

ABOVE By the spring of 1940 Britain's railway companies had supplied 25 ambulance trains for use both at home and abroad. In September 1942 the Government ordered a further 27, of which the GWR was to supply four. By September 1943 Swindon Works had completed ambulance trains Nos 32 and 33, and by January 1944 the subsequent two trains were ready. This official image taken in July 1943 shows ward car No 3209 from overseas ambulance train No 32, just prior to the whole of the train being completed. The car was converted from a Siphon G wagon and the wording 'Westinghouse Brake' painted on the end of the body confirms that this braking system had been fitted to the vehicle especially for its use overseas.

LEFT This internal view of an ambulance ward car gives a clear image of not only the ingenuity used in converting rolling stock for medical use, but also the cramped conditions endured within these vehicles. Each ward car was fitted with a tier of three beds along each side, which could be arranged for either lying down or could be folded against the wall when not in use. Note the straps around the underside of the beds and coming down the side of the ceiling, holding the beds securely in place. This appears to be a staged publicity shot judging by the smiles of the casualties who are all keen to ensure that they are captured in the shot.

ABOVE This photograph shows an interior view of a goods vehicle that has been converted into an ambulance ward car. The interior appears very basic compared to the ward car looked at earlier in this chapter and the ambulance cars converted for use during the First World War. The basic slatted bunks held up by chains look to offer little in the way of comfort, and the mesh-covered ventilation slats would have allowed more than a healthy amount of fresh air to blow onto patients.

ABOVE Great Western coach No 5189 is featured in this photograph undergoing refurbishment in the Carriage Body Shop at Swindon Works in the summer of 1946. What is particularly interesting about this image is the notice fixed to the side of the carriage, worded in French, which translated reads 'Danger; refrain from going between the buffers before stopping', which suggests that this vehicle was one of the hundreds of coaches that saw service in France during the Second World War.

TOP RIGHT In November 1941 a 56-foot Corridor Brake Composite carriage was converted at Swindon Works into a rail mobile emergency canteen. Its purpose was much the same as the road mobile emergency canteen featured elsewhere in this book, which was to provide catering facilities to company staff at places where feeding arrangements were not available following air raids. The coach, pictured here, was fully fitted out with kitchen equipment and storage facilities. Four tanks in the roof held 230 gallons of clean water, and a gas cooker and a refrigerator meant that hot, fresh food could be provided to staff during an emergency situation. The canteen was

equipped with gas lighting, but Tilley lamps were also on board should they be needed, and in order to abide by ARP regulations the windows were dressed with blackout curtains.

BOTTOM RIGHT The fear of gas attack was of paramount concern during the Second World War, as demonstrated by the mass issuing of gas masks prior to the outbreak of war in 1939. One of the responsibilities of the ARP services was to lead the decontamination and cleansing process in the event of such an attack. Mobile cleansing units were made available to the ARP service to clean people who had been exposed to gas attack, and in July 1941 the GWR converted Brake 3rd coach No 3307 into an ARP Cleansing Unit for this purpose. The van was equipped with an airlock leading to an undressing room, showers and, further along the vehicle, a dressing room stocked with fresh clothing. As can be seen in this photograph, the windows were completely blacked out and they were also made to be blastproof. This was one of 47 such units converted by the major railway companies, which were stationed at strategic locations for immediate dispatch to any station or rail depot where they were needed.

TOP LEFT A trainload of military tanks, loaded onto Crocodile G wagons, makes its way through Acton en route to the Channel ports for shipment overseas. The movement of trainloads such as this was challenging and often dangerous work for the driver and fireman, particularly during an air raid when this type of load would be a prime target for attack. However, the work had to be done and the movement of munitions and military equipment became an everyday occurrence during the war years, particularly during the build-up to D-Day when the number of special Government trains increased dramatically.

BOTTOM LEFT Three tanks are being loaded onto Rectank flat wagons that were designed and built specifically for the movement of military vehicles by rail. The 'GW' lettering on the side of the Rectank shows that the railway company owned the wagons in this image, while many others used to transport military equipment were owned by the War Department and shared between the various railway companies as and when they were needed. The careful manoeuvre of these tanks is being overseen by a number of both military and railway personnel.

ABOVE This photograph, taken at Old Oak Common on 10 April 1942, shows a 16-inch gun barrel that has been loaded onto an 18-wheel gun wagon ready for delivery. It is interesting to note the messages that have been written on the side of the barrel in chalk, presumably by members of railway staff.

ABOVE This image shows a 16-inch naval gun being carried on a set of four Pollen E wagons in March 1944. Built in the early 1900s, this Pollen E set was capable of taking 30 tons on each wagon when spread evenly. The wagons were specially adapted to carry these guns and used chocks and trestles to rest the weight of the breech and barrel along its length. The guns were loaded onto the wagons by crane inside the workshops at Swindon Works.

TOP RIGHT As well as assisting in the transportation of military goods by rail, the GWR also facilitated the war effort at its docks. This fascinating image from circa 1941 shows a Sea Hurricane being loaded onto an armed merchant ship at the GWR docks in Cardiff. Once on board, the Sea Hurricane would eventually be attached to a catapult, seen here on the deck of the ship. In the absence of a runway the catapult fired the Sea Hurricane at high speed into the air, but unless a nearby aircraft carrier or airstrip was on hand to receive a return landing the Hurricanes (their pilots having already ejected) would often ditch in the sea.

BOTTOM RIGHT Westbourne Park yard in April 1939 is the focus of this interesting pre-war image. Parts of Anderson shelters are being unloaded from a line of wagons onto a 3-ton Scammell tractor by a Ransomes & Rapier petrol-electric crane. From February 1939 Anderson shelters were distributed to households throughout the country; they were issued free to low-income households, while to those that earned more than £5 per week they were sold at a cost of £7. A total of 3.6 million Anderson shelters were issued or sold during the Second World War. From Westbourne Park yard these shelters would have been distributed to homes throughout the London area.

ABOVE This photograph of a GWR lorry was taken around 1940, and shows the delivery of historic and valuable paintings from the National Gallery in London to the disused Manod slate mine at Blaenau Ffestiniog in Wales. In the 10 days following the declaration of war on 3 September 1939 the National Gallery, with the help of the GWR Road Cartage Department, removed the majority of its paintings to safer locations in Wales. The GWR was praised by Gallery officers for its 'wonderful work' and the 'great care' with which the artworks were handled. In the next few months it was decided to store all the paintings in one location, and the Manod slate mine was the perfect choice. The GWR assisted in the relocation, which was completed by the summer of 1941.

TOP RIGHT This picture, taken in April 1941, shows five Chevrolet Thornton military trucks lined up outside the GWR's works at Caerphilly. These trucks were imported from the USA and arrived unassembled in crates; they were then assembled in full at the Works. In March 1941 the Lend-Lease scheme was enacted, a programme that allowed the USA to supply, or effectively lease, material and goods to Britain and the Allied forces. This included munitions, food, land vehicles, ships and aircraft. The trucks in this photograph have been painted in military camouflage colours and are likely destined for France.

ABOVE These rather forlorn-looking lamps appeared in an article from the April 1942 edition of the *GWR Magazine*, which looked at the daily toll of damaged and lost locomotive equipment and called upon employees to make a positive contribution to this loss and damage. During the war there was a shortage of raw materials and unnecessary repairs or replacements took their toll on resources. For example, more than 200 lamps a week were arriving at Swindon Works for repair. It was considered an employee's 'National Duty' to keep the nation's transport system running smoothly.

ABOVE This photograph was taken on 20 April 1944 and shows Chief Mechanical Engineer F. W. Hawksworth presenting a War Savings League Cup to members at Swindon Works. The National Savings Movement was set up in 1916 to help people save money as well as contributing to the war effort at the same time. During the Second World War the War Savings Campaign was introduced as part of the Movement specifically to raise funds for the war. Employees of the GWR set up savings groups as part of this campaign, with some depots and offices creating leagues. Swindon Works had a league of 42 member groups and competed for the Director Challenge Cup in their 'zealous drive' to attract new members and increase contributions.

LEFT The American flag flies from the front of the hotel at Paddington station on 4 July, American Independence Day, in 1941. At this stage the US was not involved in the Second World War, but its support for the British side was evident with the Neutrality Patrols by US warships in the waters of the western hemisphere reporting the movements of German ships to the British Navy, and the supply of money, munitions and food to support the British war effort. In return, the GWR, by flying the Star-spangled Banner, was demonstrating its spirit of comradeship with the United States. By late 1942, almost a year after America had joined the war, a close alliance between the US and the GWR was confirmed by a letter from Colonel N. A. Ryan, Chief of Transportation for the US Army, to James Milne, GWR General Manager, to thank the company for all the support it had shown to the US Army.

ABOVE Once the USA joined the war following the bombing of Pearl Harbor in December 1941, the GWR became involved in the provision of rolling stock for use by the American Army. As preparations for D-Day progressed, the US requested that ten ambulance trains be provided for the conveyance of American casualties. This image shows the official handing over of the first of these trains in a ceremony held at Swindon Works on 24 March 1943. The 14-coach train was aptly hauled by USA 'S160' 2-8-0 locomotive No 1606 and comprised six ward cars, kitchen cars, a pharmacy and operating theatre, and carriages for staff. The handover was performed by GWR Chief Mechanical Engineer F. W. Hawksworth, standing to the right of the group of uniformed American Officers, and the occasion was considered noteworthy enough for the attendance of a newsreel camera, which can just be seen on the extreme right of the photograph.

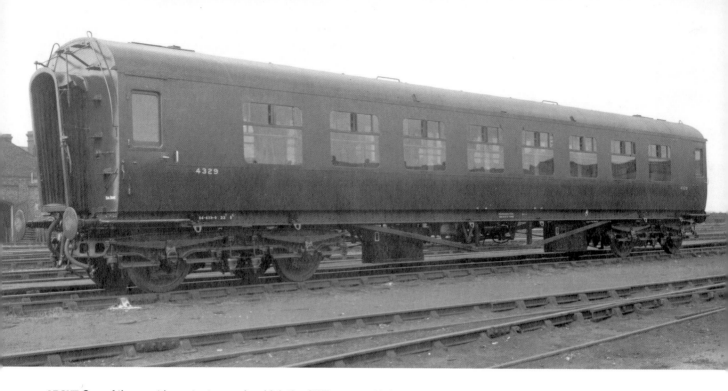

ABOVE One of the most important areas in which the GWR was asked to support both the war effort and the US Army was in the provision of what was codenamed the 'Alive' train, which was to be used by US General Dwight D. Eisenhower while in Britain making preparations for the invasion of Europe. Much secrecy surrounded both the make-up and operation of this train, although some details have emerged during the years following the war, and we know that carriage No 4329, seen here, was one of the sleeping coaches from the 'Alive' train. It is understood that the order for the train was issued in June 1942 and that many additions and improvements were subsequently made over the following years, making it a fully equipped and self-contained train from which General Eisenhower and his team could operate. During the latter years of the war the 'Alive' train travelled extensively around Britain, and in December 1944, fully equipped with bullet-proof glass, it was shipped overseas where it operated throughout France and on many occasions travelled close to the enemy line.

TOP RIGHT The GWR docks in South Wales became busy points for the arrival and departure of US troops from mid-1942 when the first American ship to arrive at the company's docks berthed at Swansea on 18 August. From that date, thousands of American soldiers passing through western ports became a common sight. This image shows a troop of US soldiers embarking on a ship at one of the South Wales docks in 1942, presumably on their way to fight with Allied forces in Europe.

Unfortunately the exact date the photograph was taken and the dock from which they are departing are not known. Not only was the mobilisation of troops from the ports a huge undertaking, but so too was the loading and unloading of US tanks, planes, trains and a whole range of other military equipment that the US military brought with it to support the Allied war effort.

BOTTOM RIGHT A troop of US soldiers are photographed here at Swansea Docks on 18 October 1943 preparing to board a special train that will take them on to their British military base. These troops had just disembarked from the American passenger ship SS *Santa Rosa* on a day that had seen more than 10,000 US soldiers arrive at the docks in Newport, Cardiff and Swansea and board 28 trains for their onward journey. Days such as this undoubtedly tested the organisational skills of the Great Western docks and railway. The arrival of US soldiers, with their chewing gum and coffee, is a well-documented part of the Second World War, but what is less well known is the invaluable help the troops gave to the ports during their time in Britain in unloading cargo from ships, particularly at a time when the GWR and other dock management companies were struggling to operate with a depleted workforce. By the time the war ended, the South Wales docks had seen more than 260,000 British and American military personnel pass through and more than 7 million tons of cargo loaded or offloaded for the war effort.

TOP LEFT From late 1942 American locomotives began to arrive at the Great Western's South Wales docks, having been shipped from America to assist Allied forces both in Britain and on the continent. Here we see 'S160' Class 2-8-0 locomotive No 1609 draped in the US and British flags having just arrived at Newport Docks. This was one of 800 'S160' Class American engines that were dispatched from Newport to railways around the country. The vast cranes for lifting cargo from ships can be seen in the background. Such was the quantity of goods being loaded and unloaded at the South Wales docks during the latter half of the war that US forces loaned 30-ton floating cranes to the docks at Cardiff, Newport and Swansea to assist with the movement of heavy cargo.

BOTTOM LEFT On 11 December 1942, for the very first time, an American-built locomotive steamed into Paddington station. Acute shortages of locomotives on the GWR network due to engines being sent overseas caused operational problems that threatened to affect the service the company could offer to both the Government and the general public. This was alleviated in part by borrowing locomotives from other British railway companies and also reinstating previously withdrawn

engines into service. In 1942, however, a number of American locomotives were shipped over to Britain to assist the domestic transport network. At a ceremony held at Paddington on this day, US 2-8-0 tender locomotive No 1604, pictured here adorned with the British and American flags, was formally handed over to Lord Leathers, Minister of War Transport, by Colonel N. A. Ryan, Chief of Transportation for the American Army, who stated that he hoped the locomotive 'will do as good work for you as British engines have done already for us.'

ABOVE The same US locomotive, No 1604, is photographed here at Swindon Works in December 1942. Many of the American engines that were shipped to Britain were actually on their way to service on the continent. However, during their stay in Britain they were put into service on the country's railway networks. The difference between US and Great Western locomotives provided challenges for locomotive crews, with the high-sided tenders causing issues at coaling stages and the single boiler water gauge leading to several boiler explosions. In total, 174 US 2-8-0s worked on GWR routes, with engine No 1604 working across the Western network from January 1943 until she was sent overseas in September 1944.

ABOVE This is an unusual inclusion in the photographic collection at STEAM, being an image of a US 0-6-0T shunting tank engine that never actually worked on the Great Western network. Nevertheless, this Class S100 engine is still worth a mention as part of the Great Western war story, as 382 of them were shipped over to Britain from America with the intention of operating them on the railways of Europe after D-Day. They arrived at the Great Western's Newport Docks from July 1942, and were towed from there to GWR sheds where their final assembly was completed and they were run in and steam tested. While the majority of the US 0-6-0s then continued on their journey to Europe, some were temporarily put to use as shunting engines at various GWR locomotive depots, and 42 were put into storage at the company's Newbury Racecourse station where they remained, unused, until 14 were acquired by the Southern Railway after the war. This image shows a rather dusty No 1940 in its black War Department livery.

TOP RIGHT This image shows the SS *St Julien* at Newport Docks following her conversion into a hospital ship, as denoted by the red cross painted on the side of her hull. The *St Julien* was one of seven GWR ships that were requisitioned for war service in the early months of the war. The company ships played a vital role in transporting troops, cargo and wounded soldiers across the English Channel. This was dangerous work for the ships and their crews, sailing over

to occupied France, often under fire from enemy guns. The evacuation of Allied troops from Dunkirk in 1940 was perhaps the most notable and dangerous mission carried out by these ships, as they were direct targets for Luftwaffe bombers as they sailed into French waters. Operation 'Dynamo', as the evacuation was known, was undertaken by a fleet of more than 800 boats and saved more than 338,000 soldiers from capture. Amazingly, no Great Western ships were lost during Operation 'Dynamo' and the fleet continued with wartime operations on behalf of the Government.

BOTTOM RIGHT The SS *St Julien* is pictured here at the Banana Dock in Dieppe during her service as a hospital ship. She was built in 1925 as a vessel to serve the GWR's Weymouth route, which she did until requisitioned by the Government on 9 September 1939 to work as a troop ship. During the following month the steamer was sent to Southampton to be converted into Hospital Ship No 29 and she began work ferrying casualties from France back to Britain, from where they would be taken by train to hospitals around the country. The *St Julien* took part in the evacuation of Dunkirk, crossing the channel six times in an attempt to reach troops, where, despite being clearly identified as a hospital ship, she came under enemy fire. She survived Dunkirk and subsequent service as a hospital ship in the Mediterranean, and at the end of the war she returned to operation on the Weymouth service.

WOMEN IN
THE LINE OF DUTY

Despite railway work being a reserved occupation during the Second World War, more than 15,000 Great Western men enlisted to fight for their country. This inevitably left huge gaps in the workforce that the company needed to fill in order to continue with both the everyday operation of the railway and the increasing amount of war work that was being contracted to it. The only option was to recruit women, which of course had happened during the First World War, so the precedent was already set and Britain's women had already proven themselves capable of stepping into the men's shoes.

Initially the GWR was somewhat reluctant to supplement its depleted workforce with female employees. Although women had been employed by the railways prior to the war in traditionally 'female' jobs such as in the laundries and sewing rooms or as telephone operators and clerks, the GWR was slow to open up opportunities throughout the organisation. The Government actively encouraged the employment of women in industry during the war, and the GWR, out of necessity, began to take on more and more women until by 1943 the *GWR Magazine* proudly announced that there were 'more than 16,000 women employed on the Great Western Railway'.

Many of the jobs that needed filling were highly skilled and physically demanding, and required the women who filled them to quickly learn complex and technical new skills. Initially the jobs given to female employees were similar to those that we saw women undertake during the First World War, including ticket inspectors, porters, and in the Refreshment Department. But it was not long before their presence was essential in the railway workshops carrying out engineering and munitions work, working on the maintenance of the permanent way, and at the company's docks. The Locomotive Department was one area where it took considerable encouragement by Great Western management to get staff shortages resolved by the employment of women. This was caused by the reluctance of shed foremen to accept women as engine cleaners and other roles within the engine sheds.

The introduction of so many women into the traditionally male-dominated railway highlighted the fact that many basic facilities for use by the female workforce were simply not in place. Throughout the GWR system ladies' cloakrooms had to be installed and in many places mess-room facilities were also provided. The company even went so far as to employ a Women's Welfare Supervisor in 1941 whose job it was to promote and protect the interests of female employees. This demonstrated that, despite its reluctance to embrace the use of women, the GWR was aware that they were vital to the functioning of the railways during the war years.

In this chapter we explore some of the varied roles that these brave, hardworking female employees undertook during the Second World War.

ABOVE Although women were employed on the railways prior to 1939, work involving the operating of heavy machinery, as shown in this photograph, was considered to be unsuitable for the fairer sex. The severe shortage of staff during the war meant that the railways had to open up male-only roles to female workers. The GWR was slow to embrace this fact, initially only allowing women to be employed in the more genteel roles within the company, and it was not until 1943 that women began to infiltrate all areas of railway employment.

ABOVE A larger group of female employees is photographed here engaged in the making of lamps at Swindon Works. The tin lamp bodies and glass lenses are neatly stacked on the workbench awaiting assembly. The mass employment of women posed many challenges for the GWR, not least in the provision of suitable facilities such as toilets and rest rooms. In 1941 a Women's Welfare Supervisor, Miss Brennan, was appointed by the GWR to advise on such matters and to champion the use of women in all areas of the organisation.

TOP RIGHT In Swindon Works some time during the latter half of the war, three women work on the riveting of a locomotive boiler in V Boiler Shop. This kind of heavy work was previously undertaken exclusively by men, but necessity during the Second World War meant that women became essential to the continued operation of the railways and the construction of new locomotives and rolling stock.

BOTTOM RIGHT Here female employees are welding the superheaters for locomotive boilers. As rail operation was essential to the war effort, so too was the maintenance of existing rolling stock and the construction of new vehicles to ensure that the railways could keep going. This was a point stressed by the Ministry of War Transport, which met regularly with GWR management to ensure that targets were being met.

LEFT A female crane operator is working alongside two male colleagues, manoeuvring a locomotive wheel set into place. What is particularly interesting to note in this image is the large expanse of roof lights that has been blacked out as a precaution against air raids. The windows were painted with a thick black paint in order to prevent light from the workshops highlighting the Works as a target for air strikes. This had the effect of turning previously light, airy shops into dark, gloomy places to work.

RIGHT AND BELOW The Road Motor Department at Slough was another area that saw the employment of women in traditionally male roles. Both of these photographs were taken on 18 April 1944 and show female mechanics involved in the maintenance of the GWR's fleet of road vehicles. Supply difficulties and the shortage of trained staff made the maintenance of the road vehicles increasingly challenging but, with the railways being the biggest operators of road vehicles, it was vitally important that road services remained fully operational. With typical GWR resourcefulness, damaged and worn parts were repaired, and when component parts were not available from specialist firms replacements were fabricated in the company's own workshops.

ABOVE Three ladies from the Permanent Way Department are pictured here at Reading in April 1943 off-loading wooden blocks from a wagon. This photograph is an official company image, with 'GWR Chief Engineers Office, Aldermaston. Photographic Department' stamped on the reverse. The photo may have been taken to show the work of women during the war, but equally it might have been taken to show joint working between the GWR and LMS, whose wagon features in the image. Inter-railway working between the railway companies was actively encouraged by the Government during the war as a means of maintaining an efficient and economic rail service, so staff and rolling stock worked across the different networks in a way that had not been seen previously.

ABOVE The Goods Yard at Cardiff Docks in September 1943 is the subject of this image featuring a group of ladies stacking boxes that have probably just been off-loaded from a goods train. Staff shortages at docks at the beginning of the war led to changes in the terms of employment for dock workers, with staff being transferred from casual to permanent contracts with guaranteed work and a minimum wage. This made the job more appealing and ensured a more reliable labour force in what was a crucial industry for the war effort. By the time this photograph was taken in 1943 more than 100 women were employed in a variety of roles at Cardiff Docks.

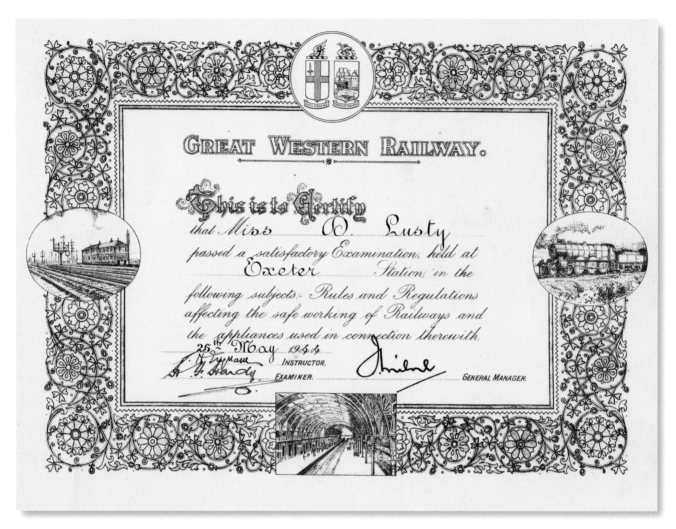

GREAT WESTERN RAILWAY.

This is to Certify

that Miss D. Lusty

passed a satisfactory Examination, held at

Exeter Station, in the

following subjects:- Rules and Regulations

affecting the safe working of Railways and

the appliances used in connection therewith.

25th May 1944

INSTRUCTOR.

EXAMINER.

GENERAL MANAGER.

ABOVE This certificate, which comes from the archives at STEAM, belonged to Miss Dorothy Lusty who was a signalwoman for the GWR at Brixham between 1941 and 1946. Only a handful of women took on this role during the war and it required the same level of knowledge and skill as a male counterpart. Examinations were an important part of the role, and this particular exam in safe working that Dorothy undertook in May 1944 shows how well-qualified some women became when employed with the company.

RIGHT This official photograph shows a ticket inspector at Paddington station checking the ticket of a passenger on board an outbound train in 1943. The famous clock located on Platform 1 can be seen looming over the roof of the carriage. Unnecessary rail travel was discouraged in order that resources could be focused on the movement of troops and goods, and the Government poster campaign asking 'Is Your Journey Really Necessary?' became a common sight at most railway stations.

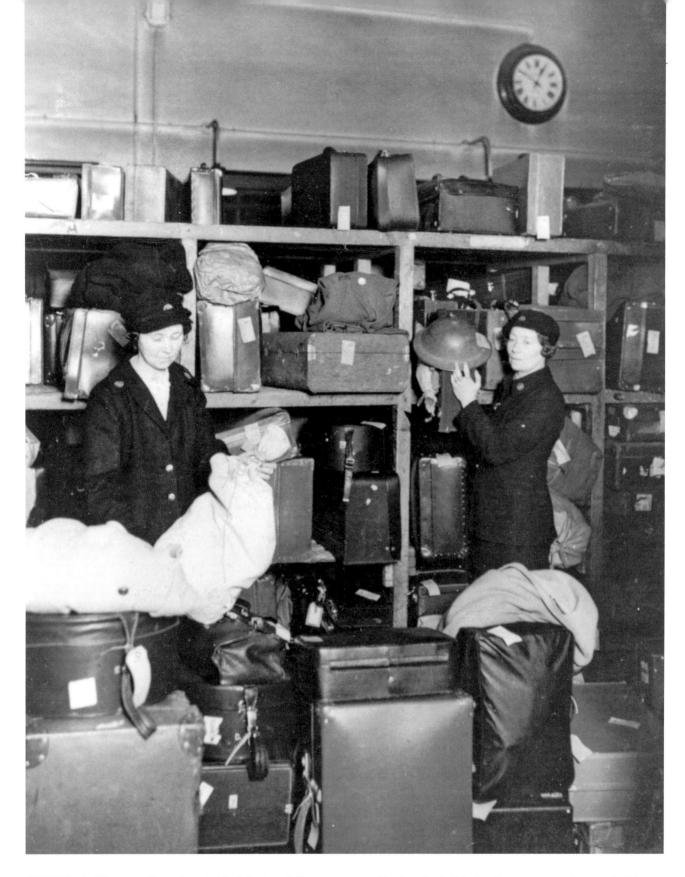

ABOVE The Left Luggage Department at Paddington station was manned by female staff during the war, as can be seen in this image taken in 1943. Such roles were regarded by the GWR as ideal for women, allowing male workers to transfer to heavier manual roles within the company. Restrictions were placed on passenger luggage from the early days of the war in an attempt to discourage travel for pleasure but, as the quantity of luggage in this photograph shows, this campaign was not completely successful. Note that the lady on the right is in the process of storing a soldier's tin helmet on the shelves behind her.

ABOVE A member of the Refreshment Department staff dispenses tea to servicemen from her platform trolley at Paddington station in this official photograph taken in 1943. Despite the fact that numerous official photographs featuring women at work were taken by the company photographer during the war, it is noticeable how much less they are featured in the *GWR Magazine* than in the previous war – an indication, perhaps, that the employment of women was no longer being regarded as a novelty.

ABOVE The series of official photographs taken at Paddington station in 1943 continues with this shot of the mobile emergency canteen, which was used to feed station staff, ARP wardens, firemen and other staff who were active during the night when the station canteen was closed. The canteen was usually manned by a driver and a female attendant and was designed so that it could move from place to place where it was most needed when air strikes affected station or depot facilities. This mobile trailer canteen was designed in the Road Transport Department Drawing Office at Slough and built at Swindon Works, and was designed with adaptable couplings so that it could be attached to

any of the company's articulated tractors. The canteen was fully equipped with water supply, cooking facilities, tea urn and storage space for emergency stocks of dried food.

RIGHT By 1943 there were more than 16,000 women employed by the GWR in all areas of the organisation's activities. In this image a female employee is seen securing two large wartime propaganda posters to an advertising board near Platform 10 at Paddington. The ladder upon which she is standing is marked 'GWR Commercial Advertising Department' and behind her, in steam, is a 'Castle' Class locomotive waiting to depart.

IT CAN NOW BE REVEALED –
AFTER THE WAR

The months and years after the war were symbolised by a spirit of recovery, rebuilding and hope for the future – but this was also a period of continued hardship and adjustment to the losses that had been suffered. The images in this chapter illustrate both the need to remember and the determination to recover that was representative of the Great Western Railway, and the country as a whole, at that time.

In a joint statement in the *GWR Magazine* for June 1945, James Milne, General Manager, and Viscount Portal, Chairman, wrote, 'We are proud of the splendid work which has been accomplished in spite of the many difficulties incidental to war conditions. We are equally proud of the large number of employees serving in His Majesty's Forces and can assure them of a welcome on their return.'

The GWR once again ensured that tribute was paid to the 794 of its men, and women, who had lost their lives in the war. A new plaque was added to the memorial at Paddington station that now honoured the sacrifice of its employees during both the World Wars. Adjustments had to be made as the company overcame the gaps in

its skilled workforce left by those who had died, while at the same time the women who had taken the place of the men in the company's workshops, stations, docks and depots had to relinquish their role to the men who returned home. The priority for the GWR was to rebuild a service that had been damaged by the war. New locomotives and rolling stock were needed, while the reintroduction of train services curtailed during the war and the development of infrastructure were all at the top of the agenda for the company in the years following 1945.

Yet major changes were around the corner for Britain's railways. Having seen how effectively the railway companies worked together under the control of the Railway Executive Committee during the war, the Government began to explore the idea of the nationalisation of the railways. And on 1 January 1948, less than three years after the end of the Second World War, the GWR and Britain's other railway companies were nationalised and taken permanently under the control of the British Transport Commission, and the Great Western Railway ceased to exist.

RIGHT Throughout the war the British Railways Press Office issued a series of booklets that outlined the 'official' story of the railways at war. This image shows the cover of the final booklet, which was published in 1945 at the end of the conflict. *It Can Now Be Revealed* does exactly what it says on the cover – it reveals, in detail, the role of the railways during the war years. Prior to this some of the details were shrouded in secrecy, especially information relating to munitions work at railway factories.

"IT CAN NOW BE REVEALED"

MORE ABOUT BRITISH RAILWAYS IN PEACE AND WAR

FULLY ILLUSTRATED

ONE SHILLING NET

1945

ABOVE On 11 November 1949 the war memorial at Paddington, which had been erected following the First World War, was again the focus of a moving ceremony when a new plaque was unveiled by former GWR General Manager Sir James Milne, which rededicated the memorial to include the Great Western men and women who fought and died in the Second World War. A casket was sealed within the memorial, alongside the one that was placed there in 1922, containing a Roll of Honour that listed the names of the 794 employees who gave their lives in the Second World War.

RIGHT This full-length image of the newly rededicated war memorial at Paddington appeared in the December 1949 edition of, by this time, the British Railways magazine. Less was made of this event than in the previous war. Indeed, throughout the Second World War the GWR Magazine did not include photographs of the fallen as it had during the years 1914 to 1919; the names of the missing and the dead were simply listed in the 'Among the Staff' section of the magazine each month.

ABOVE A group of visitors from the Australian Navy pose for this photograph on top of locomotive No 6021 *King Richard II*. The officers and sailors from HMAS *Australia* were on a visit to Swindon Works on 13 July 1945 while their ship was docked at Plymouth awaiting repairs. In this formal photograph the locomotive is decorated with both the British and Australian flags, and standing in the centre of the group in the trilby hat is the GWR Chief Mechanical Engineer F. W. Hawksworth.

TOP RIGHT The Australian Navy visitors are pictured again inside A Erecting Shop examining locomotive No 3827. Their ship, HMAS *Australia*, was heavily involved in the war effort throughout South East Asia until she was forced to withdraw for repairs in early 1945. She arrived at Plymouth on 2 July 1945 for a major refit and remained there until December of that year.

BOTTOM RIGHT With up to six months in port while their ship was undergoing repair, the group of Australian sailors, pictured here continuing their tour around Swindon Works, presumably had plenty of time to tour sites of interest around Britain. The impressive building in the background is the Pattern Store, which housed the GWR's thousands of component patterns.

LONDON GWR

"Afloat upon ethereal tides
St. Paul's above the city rides"

Davidson

LEFT This evocative poster of London was designed for the GWR by Frank Henry Mason in 1946 and shows St Paul's towering over the London skyline following the end of the war. The poster depicts the rebuilding of the city after it was ravaged by the sustained bombing campaign by the Luftwaffe in 1940 to 1941. The cranes carrying out the reconstruction work can be seen silhouetted against the sky. St Paul's Cathedral became a symbol of survival and hope during the Second World War as buildings around it were damaged during the Blitz, but the Cathedral escaped largely unscathed. The muted tones of the poster are very different from the usual vibrant style of GWR publicity material, and reflects the mood and austerity of post-war Britain.